Inspector of Irish Fisheries

Inspectors of Irish Fisheries report, 1879

Inspector of Irish Fisheries

Inspectors of Irish Fisheries report, 1879

ISBN/EAN: 9783741104473

Manufactured in Europe, USA, Canada, Australia, Japa

Cover: Foto ©ninafisch / pixelio.de

Manufactured and distributed by brebook publishing software
(www.brebook.com)

Inspector of Irish Fisheries

Inspectors of Irish Fisheries report, 1879

REPORT

OF THE

INSPECTORS OF IRISH FISHERIES

ON THE

SEA AND INLAND FISHERIES OF IRELAND,

FOR

1879.

Presented to both Houses of Parliament by Command of Her Majesty.

DUBLIN:
PRINTED BY ALEX. THOM & CO., 87, 88, & 89, ABBEY-STREET,
THE QUEEN'S PRINTING OFFICE,
FOR HER MAJESTY'S STATIONERY OFFICE.

1880.

[C.—2627.] *Price 8½d.*

CONTENTS.

535

REPORT

OF THE

INSPECTORS OF IRISH FISHERIES

ON THE

SEA AND INLAND FISHERIES OF IRELAND, FOR 1879.

TO HIS EXCELLENCY FRANCIS THOMAS DE GREY, EARL COWPER, K.G.,

&c., &c , &c.

LORD LIEUTENANT-GENERAL AND GENERAL GOVERNOR OF IRELAND.

MAY IT PLEASE YOUR EXCELLENCY,

We have the honour, in conformity with the 112th sec. of the 5th and 6th Vic., cap. 106, to submit our Report for the year 1879, being the eleventh since the Sea and Inland Fisheries of Ireland have been placed under the superintendence of this Department.

SEA FISHERIES.

The Returns received from the Coast Guard show that in 1879 the number of vessels engaged in fishing for sale belonging to this country was 5,834, with crews consisting of 20,449 men and 820 boys.

Of the above, 1,756 vessels, 6,304 men, and 421 boys, are shown as solely engaged in fishing,—the remainder, viz., 4,078 vessels, 14,145 men and 399 boys, as only partially so engaged.

These Returns, as compared with those for 1878, show an increase of 75 vessels—529 men and 14 boys engaged in the Sea Fisheries of Ireland.

We believe the foregoing figures to be as nearly correct as, under existing circumstances, it is possible to give them. The difficulty of securing reliable statistics are very great, but this has been fully referred to in our Annual Report for 1878.

It will be seen that for the last three years (viz., since we have made special efforts to secure greater accuracy in the collection of statistics), the returns show a slow but steady increase in the number of vessels and persons employed in sea fishing ; and we have little doubt, but that when the contemplated extension of pier and harbour accommodation, now about to be commenced, is carried out ; that a more decided and rapid increase may be looked for.

It is satisfactory to note that the conduct of the fishermen generally has been good ; and with the exception of an outrage committed in Bantry Bay by local fishermen upon two trawl boats—no complaints have reached us during the year.

It appears that on the 21st October two trawlers—one from Cork, the other from Dingle—had been trawling in Bantry Bay. These vessels were boarded by the crews of some local boats, their trawl cut away and their rigging damaged, and from the threats of some of the attacking party, for a time there appeared to be considerable danger that they would sink them. However, eventually, they left without doing further damage.

Great jealousy exists against strangers trawling in Bantry Bay more particularly as trammel net fishing is extensively carried on there.

A gun-boat was immediately sent to preserve order in the locality, and although for a time considerable excitement prevailed, there has been no repetition of the offence.

A number of the men who were identified as having taken part in the outrage were arraigned before the Judges at the Cork Spring Assizes. They pleaded guilty, and

A 2

threw themselves on the mercy of the Court, stating at the same time, that they had made all the reparation in their power by recovering and restoring the trawl. Under the circumstances they were released without punishment, bail only being required for their good conduct for twelve months.

On several occasions when making our Annual Reports, we have brought under notice the expression of our opinion, that very great benefit would arise if we had attached to this department a properly equipped vessel—to enable us to carry out experiments in fishing—and for the discovery of new fishing grounds.

We feel that we should neglect our duty, if we failed again to revert to the subject, and we respectfully urge it upon the consideration of your Excellency.

A vessel of the kind referred to, adapted to different kinds of fishing, and with a sufficient number of fishermen amongst the crew, skilled in all the various modes of their craft, would prove invaluable; not only in looking out for new fishing grounds off our coasts, but also in instructing the local fishermen in the latest and most approved methods of capturing the various kinds of fish.

GALWAY BAY.

. Although complaints have reached us to the effect that the trawlers ran foul of and carried away some of the fishing lines yet no complaints that the opening up of the bay for trawling has resulted in a reduced capture of fish by the line fishermen have been received, and it is understood that they have had a most satisfactory season's fishing.

If trawlers run foul of and carry away lines they should be compelled to pay for the loss and damage, and the law is sufficient to secure this if the parties aggrieved will only summon the offenders.

Trawling off the East Coast.

During the month of June we held public inquiries at Kingstown, Howth, Balbriggan, Clogher Head, Dundalk, and Newcastle, to ascertain whether or not the Bye-Laws in force should continue, or whether or not it would be advisable to repeal or modify them.

These Bye-Laws are three in number—the first, dated 10th October, 1842, prohibiting trawling in Dublin Bay.

The second, dated 14th February, 1851, prohibiting trawling within a line from the Nose of Howth to the eastern point of St. Patrick's Island (Skerries), thence to Clogher Head, thence to Dunany Point, and thence to Cranfield Point, in the County Down.

The third, dated 3rd December, 1851, prohibiting trawling in Dundrum Bay.

At the first inquiry, held at Kingstown, no evidence was brought forward, nor, indeed, was any desire manifested on the part of the trawling community, to repeal the existing restrictions in regard to Dublin Bay; and as the line fishermen, of whom there is a considerable number, attach very great importance to the maintenance of the Bye-Law, we deemed it inexpedient to make any change.

With regard to the second Bye-Law—at the inquiries at Howth, Balbriggan, and Clogher Head—those interested in trawling were strongly in favour of its repeal, and it appeared by the evidence; that outside the present limits a larger quantity of small unmarketable fish are captured, than would be in the shallower waters where trawling is now prohibited. This was explained by the statement that in easterly winds the small immature fish keep off shore to a considerable distance.

At Clogher Head strong opposition was made by the line fishermen, of whom there is a good number, against the removal of the restrictions, and they urged that if the trawl boats are permitted to cruise on the ground where trawling is now prohibited, they would be driven to the Poor House.

At inquiries of this kind the evidence is generally of an exaggerated character, and it is exceedingly difficult to ascertain the true state of things; but it was clearly shown, that before the enactment of the Bye-law of 1851 more fish were taken along the coast than since, and a larger number of trawlers were then in existence.

The Clogher trawlers generally fish from 1st April to 1st November, when most of the line men are away engaged in herring fishing, and it was shown that at certain times very good marketable fish could be taken with the trawl, which are seldom caught with line and hook.

After a very careful consideration of the subject, we came to the conclusion that it would be advisable to remove the restrictions against trawl fishing, in certain localities where trawling may be carried on with advantage. It did not appear to us that the operations of the trawl would at all seriously diminish the quantity of fish to be taken by the line fishermen; on the contrary, in other places where restrictions have been removed, it has been found that the line men have been more successful than previously, and as reported by the Royal Commissioners of 1863 on the Sea Fisheries :—

" For the community at large we believe it would be better that the line fishermen should be restricted to ground on which the trawlers cannot work, even if not quite so profitably, than that trawlers should be prohibited working on any ground which is suitable to them."

No doubt the trawlers do occasionally run foul of and carry away lines, but this will seldom happen if they are properly buoyed and marked, as in most cases the trawlers can shun avoid them.

Having come to the conclusion above referred to, we framed the following Bye-law repealing the restrictions on trawling from Howth, county Dublin, to Dunany Point, county Louth, and this Bye-law is now awaiting the decision of Your Excellency and the Privy Council.

" TRAWLING—EAST COAST.

" Bye-law.

" Whereas by a Bye-law, bearing date the 14th day of February, 1851, it was provided as follows, viz. :—

"' The use of trawl-nets is hereby prohibited at all times on any part of the coast of the counties of Dublin, Louth, and Down, within, or to the westward of the limit formed as follows, namely, by a straight line drawn from the Nose of Howth to the Eastern Point of St Patrick's Island (Skerries), in the county of Dublin, and from the Eastern Point of St. Patrick's Island (Skerries), in the county of Dublin, to Clogher Head, in the county of Louth, and from said Clogher Head to Dunany Point in the county of Louth, and from said Dunany Point to Cranfield Point, in the county of Down '

" Now, in pursuance of the powers and authorities in us vested, we do hereby repeal and rescind so much of the above recited Bye-law as prohibits trawling at all times within or to the westward of the limit formed as follows, namely, by a straight line drawn from the Nose of Howth to the Eastern Point of St Patrick's Island (Skerries), in the county of Dublin, and from the Eastern Point of St. Patrick's Island (Skerries), in the county of Dublin, to Clogher Head, in the county of Louth, and from said Clogher Head to Dunany Point in the county of Louth, and the same is hereby repealed and rescinded accordingly.

" And in lieu thereof we do hereby make and ordain the following Bye-law by which it is prohibited, and it is hereby prohibited, to use any trawl-net within the limits named above, between the Nose of Howth and Dunany Point, between the 1st day of November in each year and the 1st of May in the year following."

With regard to the third Bye-law, prohibiting trawling in Dundrum Bay, as no evidence was given in favour of its repeal, and as the local fishermen were opposed to the removal of the restrictions we did not feel that it was necessary to interfere with it.

OYSTER FISHERIES.

With reference to the public oyster fisheries nothing has occurred during the year which deserves special notice, except as regards those on the east coast, situated off the counties of Wicklow and Wexford

Having received a memorial from a large number of persons at Arklow, praying for an extension of the dredging season, to enable the fishermen to dredge during the month of May on banks alleged to contain oysters, situated outside those usually fished, and which memorial was strongly recommended by the Town Commissioners.

We deemed it advisable to apply for a Government cutter to be placed at our disposal for a short time, in order that experiments in dredging might be made under the superintendence of her officers. The allegations in the memorial set forth that oysters were to be found on these beds, that they could only be dredged in fine weather and during the long days, and that it was most desirable that this concession should be made, as, from the very unsatisfactory condition of Arklow Harbour, the boats were often unable to get out to the fishing ground, and in consequence the regular dredging season was very much curtailed.

The Lords of the Admiralty acceded to our application, and H.M. cutter King George attended at Arklow, in the early part of September last, for the purpose of superintending and noting the details of the experiments.

Arrangements had been previously made that two regular dredging boats should be in readiness for the work.

However, owing to very unsettled weather, and the disinclination of the fishermen to work without being regularly paid, dredging was carried on during only three days, in depths of water varying from fourteen to thirty fathoms. One boat only dredged.

On 4th September, with six dredges, 369 oysters were found, on 15th September, with eight dredges, 1,052 oysters, and on the 16th September, with eight dredges, 701.

They were all described as fine oysters, but no small ones or spat were found.

The experiments proved that oysters are to be found outside the grounds generally
fished, but whether in sufficient numbers to prove remunerative to fishermen, at such a
distance from the shore, would appear to be questionable.

An application of a similar nature, viz., to open the month of May for dredging, has
been again addressed to us this year, and we propose to hold a public inquiry into the
subject before determining whether or not it would be prudent to recommend any change.

The question is a very serious one, at present, oyster dredging being altogether
prohibited during May, which month is the first of the annual close season, and it is
not legal for persons to have oysters in possession in Ireland during that month,
except so far as they may be on private beds; and, although the permission sought for
only applies to beds outside those now dredged, yet, unless a proper guard could be
established, by a Government vessel being told off and stationed on the ground for the
purpose, there would be great danger of the operations being carried on on the
inshore beds, already very much less productive than they have been in former
years, it is believed in consequence of over dredging.

The subject will require to be inquired into with very great care.

The public oyster fisheries off the east coast (Arklow), produced 6,013 barrels; the
prices realized ranged from 13s. to 15s. per barrel, producing in the aggregate a sum
of about £4,473. In 1878 the take amounted to 7,325 barrels, and the price then
averaged £1 per barrel.

Oyster culture, under the licences granted by the Fishery Departments, has been
on the whole, unsuccessful, as will be seen on reference to the Appendix, in the
replies to our queries by holders of licences from this department.

The French oysters imported do not appear, generally, to have succeeded, although
there are two or three cases where, up to the present, they have thriven well. We
believe this has resulted mainly in consequence of the oysters having been imported
from Arcachon instead of Auray. The latter, wherever they have been introduced,
have done well.

There appears to be no reason why, if proper arrangements be made, and the French
system of culture adopted, the enterprise should not prove successful in this country
in localities, where, in former years, oysters were to be found.

Two new licenses have been granted in 1879 to plant oysters; none have been with-
drawn.

THE HERRING FISHERIES.

Although herrings are taken in many other places, on the Irish Coast, Howth, Arklow,
Kinsale, Greenore, Ardglass, Omeath and Warrenpoint, Kilkeel, Annalong, and Courtown
are the only places from which regular and authentic statistics have been procured.

From these places, the return of herrings, taken in 1879, was 123,977 mease.

The average price per mease at which they were sold was £1 1s., producing a total
of £139,880, as compared with 193,603, averaging £1 2s. 9d. per mease, and producing
£220,278, in 1878.

There was, thus, a decrease of 69,626 mease, and of £80,398, as compared with 1878.

It would appear that this principally affected home consumption, as the number of
boxes of 2 cwt. each, exported to London, Nottingham, Bradford, Manchester, Sheffield,
Wolverhampton, Leeds, Liverpool, and Birmingham, in 1879, amounted to 120,672,
only showing a decrease of 234 boxes, in comparison with 1878.

HERRING FISHERY, 1879.

	Boats employed, and highest number on any one day.				Total Capture.	Average Price.	Value.
	English	Scotch	Irish	Manx			
						£ s. d.	£
Howth, between 5th June and 29th Nov., 1879,	60	187	115	37	20,534	1 5 7	26,262
Arklow, between 7th June and 20th Dec., 1879,	—	—	199	—	5,153	0 18 9	4,927
Kinsale, between 10th April and 20th Dec., 1879,	35	20	210	255	9,690	1 3 8	11,422
Greenore, between 3rd June and 25th Nov., 1879,	—	25	198	93	31,099	1 5 2	39,144
Ardglass, between 1st June and 22nd Nov., 1879,	12	213	94	12	48,745	1 0 0	48,912
Omeath and Warrenpoint, between 12th June and 8th Nov., 1879,	—	—	11	35	206	1 0 8	213
Kilkeel, between 1st June and 25th Nov., 1879,	100	70	200	30	3,190	1 5 0	3,900
Annalong, between 7th June and 18th Nov., 1879,	—	—	32	—	4,000	0 15 0	3,000
Courtown,	—	—	36	—	1,500	0 16 0	1,200
					123,977	1 1 0	139,880

To the improvement of Ardglass Harbour, the increase in the number of Scotch boats, over 1878, is largely owing. Our report for 1878 having dealt with the Scotch branding system, and the inexpediency of extending it to Ireland, we have only to refer to it, for the reasons which induced us to come to this conclusion.

THE MACKEREL FISHERY.

The fishery of 1879, as judged by the quantity of fish captured proved eminently satisfactory, the gross capture, by the official returns furnished to this office amounting to 167,889 boxes, of six score each, being 75,263 in excess of the capture of the year 1878.

But the prices realized ranged very much lower than in that year. During the regular season they varied from 77s., per hundred of six score, the highest price realized, to 6s., that is between March and June, but subsequently, they were sold as low as 3s. per six score.

Thus the total sum realized amounted to only £100,452, whereas with a capture in 1878, less by 75,263 boxes, the amount received came to nearly £98,000.

It would appear that the fishermen generally were by no means satisfied with the prices received for their fish at Kinsale, and this led to some of the boats instead of landing their fish there, running for Penzance on the Cornish coast where they received much more satisfactory prices. That the prices received were not satisfactory may be inferred when it has been ascertained that the average price for a box of mackerel in Liverpool, during the season, was £1 11s. 10d., whereas the price received by the captors averaged at Kinsale only 11s. 11½d.

The buyers it is reported reaped a rich harvest.

When the new pier is built at Kinsale it is to be hoped that arrangements may be made by which the fish may be sold by auction, a practice which prevails at Howth during the herring fishing, and which secures more satisfactory prices being realized to the captors, as the buying is then open to all, and a fair market value can be obtained.

The following vessels were engaged in this fishery in 1879 :—

English and Manx,						298
Scotch,						20
Irish,						218

The net weight of the mackerel captured by our boats, taking each box to contain eleven stone of fish, would amount to 13,640 tons 19 cwt. 2 qrs. and 14 lbs.

The returns show an increase of eighteen Irish boats since 1878, not a very great increase, but still it is satisfactory to find that year by year a greater interest is being manifested in this important fishery. Since 1871 the number of Irish boats has more than doubled.

There were ten cargoes of ice received containing 5,215 tons. Fourteen hulks were employed for storing and packing—and for carrying purposes, fifteen steamers and six Jersey sloops.

Besides those of the United Kingdom there were 108 French vessels, during the mackerel season fishing off our coasts ; of these—

89 were from Bolougne,
17 were from Fecamp and
2 were from Dieppe.

The gross tonnage of these vessels amounted to 6,601 tons, and the crews numbered 2,128 men, this would give an average of over 61 tons, and 19 men to each vessel.

It is reported that all these boats are provided with steam gear, with which to haul their nets, &c., and one was provided with an auxiliary screw propeller.

The mackerel captured by the French vessels is shown by an official return, to amount to 1,046,472 kilogrammes, or according to our scale, over 1,050 tons.

The nets used are of immense length, and heavier than those used by our fishermen.

Year by year this fishing is gradually being developed further westward and northward —in 1879 considerable quantities were captured as far north as Smerwick Harbour, county Kerry. At Coulough Bay, north of Castletown-Berehaven, county Cork, an English buyer, purchased and sent away a large quantity in ice, and it is believed that he proposes to carry on more extended operations in the future.

When at Smerwick Harbour north of Dingle, in February this year, one of the Inspectors received reliable information that great quantities of mackerel and hake had been seen within two miles of the coast continuously from the commencement of the mackerel season in March. This should encourage our fishermen to continue their operations throughout the year, as by proper arrangements to ice and transport the fish to market, it is believed that the fishing would prove highly remunerative.

The great drawback to any fishing being prosecuted on an extended scale in this or any other similar locality is the great distance between the place of capture and a line of railway ; at present, the nearest station is Tralee, situate twenty-seven miles from Dingle, and about thirty-five from the fishing-ground.

THE PILCHARD FISHERY.

Up to the present with the exception of the work done by the Small Company, which had been established at Baltimore, no attempt to capture this fish on a large scale t) be cured for the Italian markets has been undertaken, and we regret to find that the operations of the Company above alluded to have not proved successful, and its affairs have been wound up and the plant sold.

Notwithstanding this, we believe that this fishery may be prosecuted satisfactorily if undertaken judiciously, and by persons with a knowledge of the localities and people.

That this was the case many years ago is abundantly proved by old histories of the county of Cork, in which reference is made to the large sums realized by the sale of this fish.

During 1879, it is reported shoals were seen off the following places :—

Dunmore, county Waterford,	.	.	.	Shoals of pilchards were seen from nine to thirteen miles from shore.
Ardmore, ,,	.	.	.	About one mile off.
Kinsale, county Cork,	.	.	.	Captured in very large quantities close in shore.
Horn Strand, ,,	.	.	.	Appeared in September and October.
Courtmacsherry, ,,	.	.	.	Do., do., do.
Barry's Cove, ,,	.	.	.	Do., do., do.
Danny Cove, ,,	.	.	.	Large shoals appeared.
Ballydonogan, ,,	.	.	.	In April and October.
Ballycrovane, ,,	.	.	.	Do., do.
Caherlinе, ,,	.	.	.	About ten miles off.
Ballydavid, ,,	.	.	.	Appeared from April to end of May, and in September, and October, about 1 mile off coast.

PIERS AND HARBOURS.

The following return has been received from the Commissioners of Public Works, showing the work done during 1879, as regards Piers and Harbours :—

1. Poul-Hurdin, Gortahis, county Donegal, . .	Preliminaries completed Works about to be commenced.
2. Malinbeg, county Donegal, . . .	Engineer's examination not yet made.
3. Port-Oriel, Clogher Head, . . .	Completed. Additional works if undertaken can be completed this season.
4. Tawney, county Donegal, . . .	Engineer's examination not yet made.
5. Muckross, county Donegal, . .	Do. do.
6. Ballysaggart, county Donegal, . .	Preliminaries completed. Works about to be commenced.
7. Scattery Island, county Clare, . .	Engineer's estimate £700. Communicated to memorialists—no reply
8. Bournapeaka, Ballyvaughan, county Clare, .	Will be completed early this year.
9. Smeeroguc or Poolally, county Galway, .	Preliminaries completed. Works about to be commenced
10. Molranny, county Mayo, . . .	Engineer's estimate sent to memorialists. Awaits presentment and contribution.
11. Scilly, Kinsale, county Cork, . .	Abandoned and Town Rock substituted.
12. Burton Port, county Donegal, . .	Preliminaries completed, and works about to be commenced.
13. North Harbour, or Kearn's Port, Cape Clear, county Cork, ...	In progress. Nearly completed.
14. Ardglass, county Down, ...	In progress. Contractor to complete work by 1st December, 1880.
15. Checkpoint, county Waterford, . .	Not yet reported on by Engineer.

An inspection of this return will show that owing to the decision of the Treasury, referred to in our report for 1878, very little has been done towards the construction of piers.

In that report we expressed the hope in reference to Ardglass Harbour, that a very dangerous ledge of rock known as the "Churn Rock," situate inside the harbour, would be removed during the progress of the present works.

This ledge of rock interferes most seriously with and limits the accommodation which the harbour is capable of affording, is a great source of danger to vessels, and has more than once been the cause of damage to them.   The cost of removing the ledge is estimated to be about £1,700.

Although we have on several occasions made strong representations as to the necessity for the removal of the ledge, which recommendations the late Lord Lieutenant, His Grace the Duke of Marlborough, endorsed, we regret to say that up to the present time we have been unsuccessful, and we see no immediate prospect of the work being done.

This is very much to be regretted, as Ardglass is one of the most important of our fishing stations, and is during the herring fishing frequented by a large fleet of boats.

The question is not simply an Irish one. It should, in our opinion be regarded as imperial ; and we submit that we are warranted in forming this opinion from the very large proportion of fishing vessels from England, Scotland, and the Isle of Man, making use of it as compared with Irish vessels ; and, in addition to our representations for the removal of this obstruction, memorials were forwarded to the authorities, not only from Ardglass but also from large numbers of Scotch fishermen.

In 1879 the number of Irish boats attending the herring fishery was 94, whilst there were 213 Scotch, 12 English, and 19 Manx; the three latter collectively being more than double the number of the local boats.

We cannot over-rate the importance of providing safe and convenient harbours wherever practicable, as without proper shelter for the boats it is not to be expected that there can be any great development of the fisheries, and although we would have been more pleased with the allocation of a much larger sum than that proposed by Government to be expended upon the construction of new piers, we anticipate considerable advantage to the fisheries if this money be expended judiciously.

In addition to our ordinary duties we had during the winter, in accordance with instructions received from the Government, to inspect and report as to the condition of the different fishery piers which had been transferred to counties under the Piers and Harbours Act, in the western and southern counties, from Donegal to Cork inclusive. The following is a list, and in the column of remarks it will be seen the condition they were in, and if it is considered advisable to have them placed in repair.

No.	County.	Name of Pier.	Remarks
1	Clare,	Ballyvanghan,	In good order.
2	,,	Bournapeaka,	Do.
3	,,	Burren,	In good order, but silting up ; requires to be cleared and deepened, and pier lengthened.
4	,,	Carrigaholt,	In good order.
5	,,	Kilbaha,	In good order, but almost useless , design defective ; a good harbour much needed.
6	,,	Liscannor,	Improvement of harbour recommended.
7	Cork,	Baltimore,	In fair order , but useless, as in a moderate S.E. gale boats could not remain ; a new harbour much required.
8	,,	Bantry,	In an extremely dilapidated condition.
9	,,	Bear Haven,	In a most dilapidated state.
10	,,	Bear Island,	In good order.
11	,,	Burrin,	Do.
12	,,	Cape Clear (Island),	North Harbour now being constructed , South Harbour in a state of ruin.
13	,,	Coulagh (Ballycrovane),	Very much out of repair.
14	,,	Courtmacsherry,	New pier in good order; old pier useless, quite dilapidated.
15	,,	Glandore,	Now undergoing repairs.
16	,,	Kinsale (Cove of),	In good order.
17	,,	Kinsale (Harbour),	Estimate prepared for new pier.
18	,,	Ring (Cork Harbour),	Could not be traced.
19	,,	Skull,	In good order, excepting one large stone displaced by a vessel.
20	Donegal,	Arranmore (Leabgarrow, Muinacreeva Cove).	
21	,,	Ballyness,	Not suitable for fishery purposes, and an extension of pier would block the channel.
22	,,	Bruckless,	In good repair.
23	,,	Bunatruhan,	New works sanctioned by Treasury.
24	,,	Bunornus,	In good order.
25	,,	Greencastle,	Harbour requires to be deepened.
26	,,	Moville,	In good order, but not used by fishermen.
27	,,	Newport (or Portnoo),	Restoration of pier necessary.
28	,,	Portenablahy,	
29	,,	Portsalon,	Almost useless for fishery purposes, and would be quite considerable extension to make it serviceable.
30	,,	Rathmullan,	In good order, but requiring some slight repairs.
31	,,	Sea View (Mountcharles),	In good order.

No	County	Name of Pier.	Remarks.
32	Donegal,	Teelin,	In fair condition.
33	Galway,	Ardfry,	In good order; wants only mooring posts, &c.; not much frequented by fishing boats.
34	„	Arran Island (Kilronan),	In good order.
35	„	Arran Island (Killeaney),	Outer part of pier requires some small repairs.
36	„	Barna,	In good order.
37	„	Barnaderg (Kealkyle, near Letterfaack).	Do.
38	„	Barnaderrig,	Do.
39	„	Bealadangan (Dangan, Pass of Bealadangan).	In very bad order, but useless for fishing boats.
40	„	Bunowen,	In fair order.
41	„	Cashla Bay,	In very bad order, and most useful for fisheries, &c.
42	„	Claddagh,	In good order.
43	„	Cleggan,	Do.
44	„	Clifden,	Do.
45	„	Dooros,	Silted up; not necessary for fisheries.
46	„	Errislannon,	Breastwork washed away; most useful for fisheries.
47	„	Greatman's Bay,	In very bad order.
48	„	Inishbofin,	In good order.
49	„	Inishshabuk,	Do.
50	„	Kilcolgan,	In bad repair, and most useful for fisheries.
51	„	Kilkieran,	In good order.
52	„	Leenane,	In fair order.
53	„	Roundstone,	In fair order.
54	„	Rosroe,	In bad repair; very useful for fisheries; should be repaired.
55	„	Spiddle,	In good repair.
56	„	Tarrea,	In good order.
57	Kerry,	Blackwater,	Do.
58	„	Cahirciveen,	Accommodation sufficient for wants of fisheries.
59	„	Castlemaine,	In good order.
60	„	Dingle,	Do.
61	„	Greenans,	In good order, excepting that coping stones are nearly all removed.
62	„	Kenmare,	In good order.
63	„	Kilmackillogue,	In good order, but a rock near end of pier interferes with vessels coming alongside.
64	„	Quay Village (Brandon Bay),	In good order, but useless, quite too short to afford shelter.
65	„	Tarbert,	Two piers here—one understood to be the property of the Steampacket Company, the other of the Shannon Commissioners. Harbour between the two piers very much silted up; piers not in good order; necessary works not considered to come under the 11th section of 16 & 17 Vic., c. 136, but to be for Harbour or Shannon Commissioners.
66	„	Ventry,	In good order.
67	Limerick,	Glin,	Do.
68	Mayo,	Achill Island (Kildavnet),	Do.
69	„	Blacksod Bay (Tarmon),	In fair repair, a few stones loose.
70	„	Blacksod Bay (Saleen),	Harbour silted up.
71	„	Belmullet,	Repairs very indifferently kept.
72	„	Blind Harbour,	No pier or slip of any description here.
73	„	Broadhaven,	Repairs very indifferently kept.
74	„	Clare Island,	In fair order.
75	„	Clew Bay (Old Head),	In good order.
76	„	Clew Bay (at Roigh),	Do.
77	„	Dooniver,	In a state of dilapidation; not much frequented by fishing boats; very little fish caught in locality.
78	„	Inishbunk (Island of),	In good order.
79	„	Muingerceva Cove (Blind Harbour).	No pier or slip of any description here; the only improvement stated to be effected was the blasting of a rock in centre of cove, and cutting away portion of the cliff above high water, to allow curraghs being hauled up.
80	„	Newport (Quay Wall),	In good order.
81	Sligo,	Roghley,	Works at present being carried out by Board of Works.

Many of these have been greatly neglected and allowed to fall into a state of dilapidation, but under 11th section 16 & 17 Vic., chapter 136, the Government has the power of causing them to be restored, charging the expenses upon the counties in which they are situated, and by which they ought to have been kept in good order.

The importance of securing facilities for transport to the great markets cannot be over-rated—they exercise the greatest influence upon the fisheries of any locality—as a rule securing to the fishermen more satisfactory prices for their fish, and bringing them in direct communication with the large buyers.

Bearing upon this subject, the following return which we have been supplied with through the kindness of Mr. Skipworth, the traffic manager of the London and North Western Railway, will show how important this is.

The return shows the number and nationalities of the fishing vessels discharging their cargoes in the neighbourhood of Greenore, Carlingford Lough, in 1875, and again in 1879.

In 1873 direct steam communication with England was first established, and its importance is shown by the remarkable increase in the number of vessels availing themselves of its advantages—the total number discharging their cargoes there in 1875 being only 412, whilst in 1879 it had increased to 3,100. Statistics on this point were taken first in 1875.

NUMBER of FISHING VESSELS that landed Fish at and in the neighbourhood of Greenore Harbour, and anchored in the roadsteads during the year 1879, as compared with 1875 :—

Month—1879.	Number of Fishing Vessels.					Remarks.
	Cornish.	Scotch.	Manx.	Irish.	Total.	
June, . . .	5	19	36	305	365	This list does not include the numerous
July, . . .	15	20	42	622	699	fleets of Fishing Craft in Carlingford
August, . . .	7	37	50	515	599	roadstead which might be reckoned
September, . . .	1	17	29	379	426	approximately at as many more.
October, . . .	—	49	178	525	752	
November, . . .	—	6	85	168	259	
Gross Total, .	28	138	420	2,514	3,100	

N.B.—On the 30th October there was 316 fishing vessels of the different nationalities in the lough, being the largest number at one time during the year 1879.

Month—1875.	Number of Fishing Vessels.				
	Cornish	Scotch.	Manx.	Irish.	Total
June, . . .	—	1	2	77	80
July, . . .	—	4	6	114	124
August, . . .	—	10	6	79	95
September, . . .	—	6	4	56	66
October, . . .	—	1	2	44	47
Gross Total, .	—	22	20	370	412

REPRODUCTIVE LOAN FUND.

Reports from the Inspectors with regard to the proceedings for 1879, will be found at pp. 20, 21, 22, 23, and 24.

The total amount available for 1879 was £6,834. The amount applied for was £13,663 1s., the applications numbered 668, from 1,149 persons.

Three hundred and forty-eight loans, comprising 519 borrowers for £5,854, were recommended—7 loans were cancelled as not perfected for £153. Instalments in 9 cases not taken up—£88. The amount actually advanced therefore amounted to £5,613.

In the County Limerick £625 was available, but no loan was applied for.

In Leitrim, £349 available—there were only two applications in this county for loans, and they could not be recommended.

In the five years since the Act has been in operation, up to 31st December last, there have been 1,420 loans actually issued for a total of £25,212 10s., and up to that date repayments have been received amounting to £15,424 1s. 4d.

The amount overdue, as well as it can be ascertained up to the present date, is £535 18s. 9d. This is much in excess of last year, but when the state of the country during 1879 is taken into consideration, it is considered that the instalments generally have been fairly paid.

Further, we believe that a considerable portion of the sum shown as overdue, has been actually recovered under proceedings taken by the Sessional Crown Solicitors, &c., from some of whom returns have not been yet received.

We believe that most of what is still overdue will be repaid.

STATE OF THE SEA FISHERIES.

DUBLIN DIVISION.
From Howth to Greystones, both Stations inclusive.

According to the Coast Guard Returns, there are in this division 185 fishing craft, with 718 men, 101 boys employed in same, compared with 193 vessels and boats, with 723 men, and 104 boys, in 1878.

Trawling, long and hand lines, herring nets, and draft nets are the means of capture. Herring, mackerel, cod, ling, plaice, joie, turbot, whiting, and other fish are taken.

Lobsters and crabs are taken at Bray Head, and between Dalkey and Bullock. About 3 dozen lobsters, and 6 dozen crabs, a week, during the season, were caught.

The conduct of the fishermen throughout the district was good.

No part of the division is unguarded.

Oyster Fisheries.

Oysters are dredged for between the Nose of Howth and Bowles Lighthouse; but the supply is decreasing. From the oyster beds of Clontarf, about £450 worth of oysters were sold between 1st September and the 8th of October.

The Sutton oyster beds have not produced any oysters, though in 1878 £2,852 1s. 6d. worth were sent to market.

ARKLOW DIVISION.
From the Breaches, County Wicklow, North, to the Sluices, near Cahore, County Wexford, South, a length of 56½ miles.

No portion of this division unguarded.

The Coastguard Returns show as employed in the fisheries during 1879, 341 vessels, 1,258 men, and 35 boys, which, as compared with our report of last year, would give an apparent decrease of 4 vessels, of 89 men, and an increase of 32 boys.

Of the boats 11 were of the first class, 211 second, and 59 of the third.

The fish principally taken are herrings, cod, oysters, and trawl fish. Mode of fishing, nets, lines, dredges, and trawls.

There were 6,013 barrels of oysters taken from the banks. The price per barrel ranged from 13s. to 15s.

From one ground it is reported that the spatting was much the same as in 1878. In the Arklow ground the report is unfavourable.

In the early parts of October large shoals of sprats appeared at Courtown, but the fishermen were not provided with any proper net with which to capture them.

The herring fishery was very unproductive. The Inspecting Commander of the division expressed his belief that the shoals passed by earlier in the season than usual, and consequently the lessened capture.

It is much to be deplored that in this division the harbours are very bad, and we regret to hear that the project to improve the harbour at Arklow has, at any rate, for the present, been abandoned.

The conduct of the fishermen has been good.

WEXFORD DIVISION.
From the Sluices near Cahore to Bannow Bay.

The Harbour of Wexford, from Rosslare to Raven point, is unguarded, being under the control of the Customs authorities.

In this division there are 153 boats, 574 men, and 6 boys engaged in sea-fishing. Of these 9 are first class boats, 133 second, and 11 third.

Solely engaged in fishing, 92 boats, 362 men, and 6 boys; partially, 61 boats, and 212 men. Fish generally captured—Herrings, mackerel, cod, bream, conger, pollock, &c., and considerable quantities of crabs and lobsters.

The modes of fishing are drift and trawl nets, hand and long lines.

Shoals of mackerel appeared off the coast between September and November.

Lobsters and crabs of fine quality were captured in great numbers around the Saltee Islands, and generally between this and the entrance of Wexford Harbour considerable numbers were taken. The fishing of 1879 is reported as having been very good.

The fishermen are reported as well behaved. Nothing especially deserving note has occurred during the year.

Unfortunately off some parts of this coast the fishermen are not provided with proper nets for the capture of fish, if they had been it is reported that large quantities of mackerel might have been taken.

WATERFORD DIVISION.

From East Bank of Bannow Ferry to Ballyvoile Head, north of Dungarvan Harbour.

This division extends along the coast for a distance of 62½ miles, all of which is guarded; but in the estuaries the following portions are unguarded:—

From Oyster Point to Wellington Bridge, 5 miles; from Ballyhack to Fisherstown, 8 miles; from Glass House to Rochestown, 7 miles; from Churchpoint to Blackrock, 10 miles; total 30 miles.

In the division there are 127 boats, 338 men, and 18 boys employed in the sea fisheries—13 first class boats, 87 second class, and 27 third class.

Of the above there are solely engaged in fishing, 14 boats, 42 men, 13 boys; partially so engaged, 113 boats, 296 men, 5 boys.

The fish principally taken are plaice, soles, turbot, brill, bream, cod, hake, ling, mackerel, whiting, and sprats, and occasionally herrings in large quantities.

The modes of fishing are trawling, seining, long-lines, hand-lines, &c.

The supply of lobsters and crabs is stated to have been good.

An improvement is reported in the oyster beds.

It is reported that quantities of bream, cod, whiting, and mackerel were seen, but the take was not large owing to the want of proper gear for their capture.

The fishermen are reported to have been orderly and well conducted.

YOUGHAL DIVISION.

From Ballyvoile Head, near Dungarvan, to Ballycottin; a distance of 56¼ miles.

Unguarded:—From Tullacort Point to Ballyvoile Bridge, two miles; from Mine Head, East, to Corrin River, West, six and three-quarter miles; from Goat Island to Ferry Point, five miles; from Glanwilliam to Ballycrivane, five miles; total, 18¾ miles.

The Coast Guard returns show as engaged in the sea fisheries 130 boats, 551 men 16 boys, viz.:—7 first class boats, 77 second class, and 46 third class. Of these 24 boats, 92 men, and 1 boy are shown as solely engaged in fishing, and 106 boats, 459 men, and 15 boys only partially so engaged.

Hake, cod, ling, plaice, soles, mackerel, bream, whiting, and large quantities of sprats have been taken.

Large shoals of mackerel, pilchards, and sprats in September and October.

Inadequate means for the capture of mackerel.

Large quantities of lobsters and crabs were taken in the season.

The fishermen reported as very orderly.

QUEENSTOWN DIVISION.

From Garryroe, in Ballycottin Bay, West, to Lane's Cottages, Ringabella Point, East. Length of coast, 110 miles.

Unguarded portion of division:—All the estuary of Cork Harbour, from and including Queenstown to the City of Cork.

The returns show that 255 boats, 714 men, and 73 boys were engaged in the sea fisheries in 1879, viz.:—6 first class boats, 120 second class, and 129 third class. Of these 110 boats, 386 men, and 25 boys were solely engaged in fishing, and 145 boats, 328 men, and 48 boys only partially so engaged.

Fish generally captured—Turbot, sole, plaice, conger, mackerel, hake, cod, pollock, whiting, bream, gurnard, sprats, and oysters.

The fishing is by means of trawls, long lines, hand lines, and seines.

Lobsters and crabs were taken, but not in any great quantity.

The fishermen are reported orderly. Nothing of any importance has occurred since report for 1878.

KINSALE DIVISION.

From Myrtleville Point, East, to Galley Head, West; a distance of 110 miles.

Unguarded portions :--From Barry's Head to Flat Head (Oyster Haven) 1¾ miles; from Muckross to Virgin Mary Point, Dunny Cove, 3 miles 180 yards; total 4 miles, 1,500 yards.

In 1879 there were 346 boats, 1,655 men, and 91 boys reported to have been engaged in the sea fisheries, viz. :--61 first class boats, 120 second class, and 165 third class. Of these 100 boats, 567 men, and 43 boys were solely engaged in fishing, and 246 boats, 1,088 men, and 48 boys as only partially engaged.

The fish found in the greatest quantities off this division are mackerel, herring, sprats, pilchards, bream, pollock, cod, hake, soles, whitings, and scad, and a few oysters.

Very large shoals of mackerel, herrings, pilchards and scad, off the coast this year, in some places quite close in shore. The capture of mackerel and herrings is generally satisfactorily accomplished, and very large quantities have been taken, but although there has been an abundance of pilchards, the take has been small. Some of the Coastguard officers report that more would be taken if Suck seines were introduced.

A fleet of over 100 French luggers attended the mackerel fishing in 1879, and they captured large quantities. It is considered that it would be of advantage if a French cruiser were put off the coast during the mackerel season to maintain order amongst the fishermen. These luggers are much larger than our boats and the crews much more numerous. In case of disputes, therefore, they would be more easily settled by a French Government Officer, and no doubt the presence of such a vessel would tend to prevent causes of complaint arising.

Lobsters and crabs were taken in fair quantities, and the supply is said to be increasing.

In last report mention was made that application had been made with the view of having the Storm Drum Signals established at Kinsale—this has been accomplished, and is in working order at Summer Cove, Kinsale.

Fishermen throughout the division are reported to have been well behaved.

SKIBBEREEN DIVISION.

From Galley Head to Snave Bridge—about 170 miles.

Unguarded about 70 miles, viz., Three Castles Head to Carberry Island, Carberry Island to Snave Bridge; from Rinks Castle to Ballydehob, besides the Islands of Clear, Sheskin, Ringarogy, Long, Castle, Horse, and other smaller ones, occasionally visited.

The returns from Coastguard show that in 1879 there were 354 boats, 1,332 men, and 20 boys employed in the sea fisheries; of these 67 boats, 343 men, and 6 boys, have been solely engaged in fishing; and 287 boats, 989 men, and 14 boys, partially engaged.

Fish generally taken are cod, ling, mackerel, hake, pollock, bream, pilchards, and scad.

Modes of fishing—seines, hand and long lines, trawls, drift nets, and trammels.

Considerable quantities of lobsters have been taken in this division, but the capture of lobsters and crabs is reported not to have been large.

The fishermen reported to have been well behaved throughout this division.

CASTLETOWN DIVISION.

From Kenmare Bridge to Snave Bridge, Bantry Bay.

A considerable portion of the coast in this division is unguarded, viz. :—From Carriglass to Snave Bridge, 16 miles; Clanderry Head to Kenmare, 14 miles; Cod's Head to Ardolaggan Point, 4 miles; Garrinish Bay to Dursey, 6 miles; Dursey Head to Pulleen, 7 miles.

The returns show that in 1879 there were 180 boats, 755 men, and 56 boys, engaged in the sea fisheries, viz, solely engaged in fishing, 1 boat and 2 men; only partially engaged, 179 boats, 753 men, and 56 boys.

The fish in general frequenting the coast are mackerel, pilchards, herrings, cod, ling, hake, pollock, whiting, &c.

Modes of capture—seines, herring nets, long lines, and hand lines.

The fishing during the year has not been as good as during the year 1878, but off the Dursey Island it is reported that large quantities of mackerel were taken late in the season.

The fishing in this division has not, on the whole, been prosperous.

The French mackerel luggers appear to have done well, however— the takes averaging from 3,000 to 20,000 fish in one night's fishing; and one boat in one night captured 60,000.

Pilchards were seen in large shoals off the Allihies ground, but the fishermen were not provided with proper means for their capture.

A few lobsters were taken.

The fishermen are reported to have been quiet and orderly.

KILLARNEY DIVISION.

From Kenmare Bridge, south, to Blennerville Bridge, near Tralee, north.

Length of coast line, 281 miles. Unguarded, 56 miles, viz. :—Inch to Castlemaine, 14 miles ; Slea Head to Clogher Head and the Blaskets, 8 miles ; Brandon Creek to Blennerville and Mahareos, 34 miles. Total, 56 miles.

By the Coastguard returns there were 350 boats, 1,483 men, and 4 boys, engaged in the sea fisheries, viz. :—Solely engaged in fishing, 82 boats and 245 men ; partially engaged, 268 boats, 1,238 men, and 4 boys.

The kinds of fish generally captured are—turbot, soles, bream, brit, plaice, cod, ling, hake, pollock, shad, mackerel, pilchards, &c.

Fish it is reported were generally scarce throughout the district during 1879.

Large shoals of mackerel and pilchards were seen off Ballydavid Guard during the greater part of the year ; and although the fishing throughout the division has not been good, yet off this Guard considerable quantities have been captured. Quantities of herrings, mackerel, and pilchards were seen, and the captures were considerable.

It is believed that Linerwick Harbour could with great advantage be made a most profitable fishing station—if fishings were undertaken there upon a larger scale.

A considerable quantity of lobsters were taken during the year.

The fishermen are reported as orderly and well behaved.

BALLYHEIGUE DIVISION.

From Blennerville, County Kerry, to Foynes, County Limerick.

During 1879, 86 boats, 247 men, and 4 boys were employed, as compared with 81 boats, 236 men, and 3 boys, in 1878. Of the boats, 9 second-class were solely engaged in fishing ; 1 first-class, 24 second-class, and 52 third-class were partially engaged in fishing.

Very little fishing is carried on in this division.

Long lines and drift nets are the modes of capture.

Herring, mackerel, and whiting are the fish caught.

Lobsters were very scarce this year.

Large shoals of herrings appeared during August and September, five miles out, especially off Beale.

The conduct of the fishermen was orderly.

The extent of coast is about 75 miles, of which about 48 are unguarded.

SEAFIELD DIVISION.

From Cancapple Head to Ballymacrennan.

During 1879, 119 boats, 293 men, and 6 boys, were employed in fishing, as compared with 155 boats, 411 men, and 4 boys, in 1878. Of the boats solely engaged in fishing, there were 15 third-class, and 42 men ; and partially engaged, 1 second-class, and 103 third-class boats, with crews amounting to 251 men and 6 boys. This shows a decrease of 36 boats and 118 men.

Nets and lines are the modes of capture.

Herring, cod, ling, mackerel, and other fish are taken.

Lobsters and crabs were captured between Loophead and Kilcredane Point, 45 dozen of the former, and 62 dozen of the latter.

From 1,200 to 1,500 lobsters were taken in the locality of Mutton Island.

Goleen, to which I referred in last report, as a place where a harbour could be advantageously made, at a small expense

The fishermen throughout the division are orderly.

The extent of the coast line is about 112 miles, of which about 71 are unguarded.

GALWAY DIVISION.

From Canamallagh Point, County Clare, to Mace Head, County Galway.

During 1879, 496 boats, 1,391 men, and 22 boys were employed, as compared with 443 boats, 1,103 men, and 34 boys, in 1878. Of these solely engaged in fishing were 10 first-class boats, 34 men and 10 boys; 4 second-class boats, and 16 men; and 125 third-class boats, 290 men, and 8 boys. There has been a considerable increase in the number of boats and men, both solely and partially engaged in fishing; this increase amounts to 56 vessels and 203 men partially engaged fishing in second-class boats, and 71 vessels, 160 men, and 8 boys solely engaged in fishing in third-class boats. There is a decrease of 72 vessels, 68 men, and 8 boys, partially engaged in fishing in third-class boats. This leads to the conclusion that fishing is more profitable and more eagerly pursued by the coast population than formerly.

Long lines, hand lines, and nets are the modes of capture.

It is stated that large shoals of mackerel show in the bay, but few are taken, from want of proper means of capture. Whiting are plentiful. Cod, ling, hake, pollock, and other fish have been more abundant, and large takes have been made.

Lobsters and crabs are taken in large quantities.

At Glanina and Murrough, 7 boats caught about 2 dozen lobsters per boat, a week. About 8,000 lobsters were taken between Costello Bay and Myniah Island.

Some disputes have taken place among the fishermen, principally from trawlers injuring the lines of the line fishermen. Generally the conduct of the fishermen has been good.

CLIFDEN DIVISION.

From Mason Island, County Galway, to Doaghbeg, County Mayo.

In 1879, 565 boats, 1,956 men and 14 boys were employed, as compared with 657 boats, 1,865 men and 48 boys, in 1878.

All the boats, which were only partially engaged in fishing, consisted of 231 second-class, and 334 third-class. This shows a decrease of 92 boats, in the division.

The modes of capture are hand lines, nets, and spillets.

Cod, ling, bream, congers, skad, mackerel, pollock, and other fish, are taken.

Lobsters were taken to the amount of 2,106 dozen, off Roundstone Station; about 200 dozen in Killery Bay; and a few in other places.

There are no professional fishermen in the division; but anyone who owns a boat uses it for fishing, when he has nothing else on hand.

The extent of coast is 262 miles, of which about 191 miles are unguarded.

KEEL DIVISION.

From Doaghbeg, to Doona, County Mayo.

In 1879, 53 boats, 97 men and 5 boys were employed in fishing, as compared with 57 boats, 122 men and 4 boys in 1878.

All the boats were third class, and only partially engaged in fishing.

Cod, whiting, bream, pollock, ling, conger, turbot, and other fish are taken. Lobsters and crabs were taken in small quantities.

The fishermen are orderly and peaceable.

The extent of coast is about 180 miles, of which none is unguarded.

BELMULLET DIVISION.

In 1879, 174 boats, 395 men and 5 boys were employed in fishing, as compared with 183 boats, and 505 men in 1878.

All the boats are third-class, and only partially engaged in fishing.

Mackerel, herring, whiting, turbot, cod, ling, and other fish are captured.

Lobsters are taken, in some portions of the division, but no accurate returns have been obtained.

The conduct of the fishermen has been excellent.

The extent of coast is about 73 miles, of which about 38 are unguarded.

BALLYCASTLE (Co. Mayo) DIVISION.

From Brandy Point, to Gap of Bartragh, Killala.

In 1879, 118 boats, and 537 men were employed, as compared with 151 boats, and 561 men in 1878. The boats were all of the third-class, and only partially engaged in fishing.

The modes of capture are nets, hand lines, and spillets.

Mackerel, herring, and, in small quantities, whiting, gurnet, and pollock, are taken.

Lobsters were taken between Crevagh Head and Ross Point, in Killala Bay, to the amount of 1,500 or 2,000.

Crabs were captured in large quantities here.

The conduct of those engaged in fishing has been orderly and quiet.

The extent of coast is about 59 miles, of which about 17 is unguarded.

POLLENDIVA DIVISION.

From Ballina West, to Coney's Island, Co. Sligo.

In 1879, 59 boats, 230 men and 12 boys were employed in fishing, as compared with 46 boats, 165 men and 7 boys in 1878.

Of the boats, 12 third-class, with 33 men and 11 boys, are solely engaged in fishing; and 47 boats, with 197 men and 1 boy, partially so.

The modes of capture are nets, and hand and long lines.

Herring, mackerel, sole, whiting, turbot, haddock, cod, and pollock are taken.

Lobsters were captured in quantities, from Enniscrone to Lacken– about 1,000 dozen, during the year. From Pollocheeny Rocks to Lenedon Point, 50 to 60 dozen were captured. From Easkey to Dunmoran, 360 dozen were taken, during six months.

The fishermen are very orderly.

The extent of coast is about 54 miles, of which no part is unguarded.

Oyster Fisheries.

The public bed extending from Ballingty Point, to Mr. Verschoyle's private oyster bed, is about half a mile in length, by 150 yards. The four boats working this, during the year, only realized about £10—not enough to pay their expenses. There was no spatting this season.

SLIGO DIVISION.

From Strandhill Barracks, to Donegal Abbey.

In 1879, 140 boats, 572 men and 6 boys were employed, as compared with 139 boats, 577 men and 8 boys in 1878. Of the boats, 1 was first-class, 14 were second-class, and 19 third-class, solely engaged in fishing; and 13 second-class, and 93 third-class, partially so engaged.

Nets, long lines, and hand lines are the modes of capture.

Cod, ling, herring, plaice, turbot, sole, mackerel, and other fish are taken.

Lobsters have been captured, to the amount of 360 dozen, in the Rockley Station. About 1,260 dozen were captured, from Tullaghan to Streedagh, and off Innismurry Island. About 40 barrels were taken at Rostrowlagh and Bormeatroohan. ..

The conduct of the fishermen has been orderly.

The extent of coast is about 80 miles, of which about 50 miles are unguarded.

Oyster Fisheries.

The oysters on the public bed in the Sligo river have greatly decreased. The same observation applies to private oyster beds in this place. About £200 worth were sold from the private beds within Rockley Coast Guard Station.

KILLYBEGS DIVISION.

From Donegal Quay to Lower Ferry (Gweebara River), Donegal.

There were, in this division, in 1879, 165 boats, employing 841 men, and 91 boys, as compared with 168 boats, 783 men, and 58 boys, in 1878.

Nets, and long and hand lines are the means of capture.

Herring, mackerel, whiting, cod, and other fish are taken. In some portions of the district, herring and mackerel were not captured in quantities, as they appeared, from

C

want of adequate means on the part of the fishermen ; whose boats and gear were insufficient for the purpose.

Lobsters and crabs were caught in considerable quantities, near Teelin, and Malinmore. In the neighbourhood of Portnoo 100 dozen a week have been taken. Great want is here felt, by the fishermen, of sufficient harbour accommodation, and the re-building of Portnoo Pier is urgently required.

The fishermen are very orderly.

The extent of coast line is 153 miles, of which about 50 miles are unguarded.

GUIDORE DIVISION.

From Gweebara Bar to Mullaghdoo.

There were, in this division, in 1879, 76 boats, employing 185 men, and 16 boys, as compared with 42 boats, 133 men, and 16 boys, in 1878.

Long and hand lines, and nets, are the means of capture.

Shoals of mackerel and herring were seen, occasionally, during the summer, round the islands of Gola, Inishman, and Inishsirrer, but very few were captured ; as the people are very poor, and would require a larger class of boats and nets.

Lobsters and crabs were taken in large quantities, off the islands of Arranmore, Gola, &c. Want of adequate means of exportation, however, causes great loss to the fishermen, as the lobsters and crabs are often lost, in hot weather, from this reason. About £1,400 worth, however, were sold, in the district, during the season.

The conduct of the fishermen was very good.

The extent of coast line is 34 miles, of which about 12 miles are unguarded.

RATHMULLEN DIVISION.

From Lough Swilly to Bloody Foreland.

There were in this division, in 1879, 187 boats, employing 476 men and 46 boys, as compared with 186 boats, 335 men, and 23 boys, in 1878.

The modes of capture are hand and long lines.

Cod, ling, flounders, haddock, and other fish were taken, but not in any considerable quantity, this year.

Lobsters and crabs were principally taken about Horn Head, and Dunree and Lennan Bay. In the former locality about 300 lobsters and 400 crabs were taken ; and, in the latter, about 40,000 lobsters and crabs.

The want of harbour accommodation, and of sufficient boats and gear, is greatly felt all throughout this district.

The fishermen of the district are orderly and peaceable.

The extent of coast line is 120 miles, of which about 56 are unguarded.

Oyster Fisheries.

There is an oyster bed at Fort Stewart, from which £20 worth were sent to Liverpool.

MOVILLE DIVISION.

From Carrickabraghy to Downhill, county Derry.

There were, in this division, in 1879, 229 boats, with 830 men, as compared with 256 boats, with 951 men and 4 boys, in 1878.

Hand and long lines are used in the capture of fish.

Turbot, cod, bream, whiting, and other fish are caught.

Lobsters and crabs were taken in considerable quantities. Between Lenon Bay and Dariff Head, 150 dozen lobsters, and between Matin Well and Dunaff Head 1,500 dozen crabs were taken. About 11,250 crabs and lobsters were taken in the localities of Portnasantally and Portalea ; and about 1,000 lobsters, and 1,500 crabs in other places.

The conduct of the fishermen has been very orderly this season.

The extent of coast line is 122 miles, of which 64 are unguarded.

BALLYCASTLE DIVISION.

From Downhill, county Londonderry, to Jenny's Bridge, county Antrim.

There were 153 boats, 271 men, 7 boys employed, in 1879, as compared with 140 boats, 270 men, and 4 boys in 1878.

Draft nets, long and hand lines, are used.

Mackerel, pollock, gurnet, skate, herring, turbot, sole, cod, and ling are taken.

Lobsters and crabs are taken in numbers between Renbane Head and Fair Head. Here about 1,250 lobsters and 3,070 crabs were captured.

The fishermen are very orderly.

The extent of coast line is about 65 miles, of which about 13 are unguarded.

CARRICKFERGUS DIVISION.

From Jenny's Bridge to Fort William Park, near Belfast.

In this division, 61 boats, 119 men, and 3 boys were employed, in 1879, as compared with 51 boats, 114 men, and 4 boys, in 1878.

Seines, long lines, hand lines, rods, drift nets, herring nets, and trawls are the modes of capture. The good trawling all over Belfast Lough is much availed of.

Large shoals of herring and mackerel appeared off the coast in August and September, from half a mile to three miles off shore, near Portmuck and Whitehead Stations, but none were captured, from want of adequate means.

Cod, ling, pollock, and other fish are taken.

Lobsters and crabs are taken principally in Carnlough and Glenarm Bays—about 3,000 lobsters and 6,000 crabs during the year.

The fishermen are very well conducted.

The extent of coast line is about 49 miles, no portion of which is unguarded.

Oyster Fisheries.

Oysters are taken all over Belfast Lough.

There is one public bed, about one mile in extent, S.S.E. from Whitehead. About £1,000 was realized during the year from the oysters taken.

DONAGHADEE DIVISION.

From Kinnegar to Newcastle Quay.

During 1879, 131 boats, 461 men, and 14 boys were employed, as compared with 123 boats, 390 men, and 28 boys, in 1878.

Hand lines, long lines, drift nets, and seine nets are the modes of capture, with trawling, in Belfast Lough.

Herring, cod, plaice, whiting, and pollock are taken.

About 2,000 lobsters and a smaller quantity of crabs were captured.

The fishermen are orderly and peaceable.

The extent of coast line is 44 miles.

STRANGFORD DIVISION.

From Newcastle Quay to Sheepland Head.

In 1879, 108 boats, 203 men, and 19 boys were employed, as against 107 boats, 189 men, and 10 boys, in 1878.

Nets and hand lines are the modes of capture.

Herring, mackerel, cod, pollock, and whiting are taken.

Lobsters and crabs have only been taken in small quantities throughout the season.

The fishermen have been well conducted.

The extent of the coast line is 26 miles.

NEWCASTLE DIVISION.

From Sheepland Head to Riverfoot, Kilkeel.

During 1879 there were employed in this division 133 boats, 621 men, and 39 boys, as compared with 157 boats, 642 men, and 33 boys, in 1878.

Trammel nets, hand lines, and long lines are the modes of capture.

Turbot, whiting, mackerel, pollock, ling, cod, and other fish are caught.

The Ardglass herring fishery is referred to elsewhere. The improvement in the harbour, adding to the safety of the herring fleet, will give increased impetus to the fishery.

Lobsters and crabs are not taken in large quantities, except between Blackrock and Riverfoot, where about 4,000 lobsters and 6,000 crabs have been captured.

The fishermen are very orderly.

The extent of the coast is about 42 miles, no part of which is unguarded.

CARLINGFORD DIVISION.

From Riverfoot, Kilkeel, to Maiden Tower, Drogheda.

In 1879, 267 boats, 904 men, and 70 boys were employed, as compared with 266 boats, 876 men, and 68 boys in 1878.

The modes of capture are nets and long lines.

Herring, mackerel, cod, and plaice are taken.

Lobsters and crabs, except in the neighbourhood of Greenore, are not taken in any quantity. About 250 of each, per week, for 34 weeks, are reported as having been taken here.

The Carlingford Station continues to be the exception to the general reports concerning the orderly conduct of the fishermen.

The extent of coast is about 86 miles, of which none are unguarded.

Oyster Fisheries.

The oyster beds of C. O. Woodhouse, Esq., have been largely stocked.

The public oyster fisheries are on the decline.

MALAHIDE DIVISION.

From Laytown to Baldoyle.

In 1879, 93 boats, 452 men, and 21 boys were employed, as compared with 112 boats, 538 men, and 40 boys, in 1878.

The modes of capture are trawling, long lines, hand lines, and herring nets.

Herring, turbot, plaice, cod, and ling are taken.

Lobsters and crabs are taken largely, between Point Lane and Tower Lane, near Loughshinny Station. About two dozen per week of lobsters are taken; and great quantities of crabs.

The conduct of the fishermen has been good.

The extent of coast is about 26 miles, none of which is unguarded.

IRISH REPRODUCTIVE LOAN FUND.

MAJOR HAYES' REPORTS FOR THE COUNTY OF CORK AND THAT PART OF THE COUNTY OF KERRY LYING BETWEEN DURSEY ISLAND AND BALLYDAVID HEAD.

COUNTY CORK.

Amount available for 1879, £951. Eighty-six applications were received for £2,552. Of these 42 were recommended, 1 was declined, and 41 were issued for the full sum available.

Of the instalments over due, amounting to £92 7s. 6d., all with the exception of three became due in 1879, clearly showing that the failure to meet engagements has been caused by the state of distress prevailing during that year.

In consequence of extra press of work during 1879, I have been unable thoroughly to investigate the expenditure, but as far as I was able to inquire the money generally had been fairly expended.

COUNTY KERRY.

Amount available £2,272. There were 155 applications for loans in that part of the county situated in my division.

The amount applied for was £3,523. After investigation I was able to recommend 104 for a total sum of £1,923.

As far as I have been enabled to investigate the application of the loans, I believe the money has in most cases been fairly applied.

The total amounts advanced year by year in loans in this part of the county since the Reproduction Loan Fund Act has been in force are as follows :—

	No of Loans.	Amount Advanced.	No	Instalments Due, but still unpaid.		
		£		£	s.	d.
1875,	94	2,315	5	49	12	0
1876,	19	1,067	6	37	3	4
1877,	6	114	4	38	3	2
1878,	87	2,261	7	22	8	0
1879,	102	1,923	4	8	4	6
	308	£7,680		£155	11	0

Nearly all the money advanced to Kerry has been in this portion of the county, and up to the 23rd instant, it appears by a memorandum received from the Office of Public Works, repayments have been made amounting to £5,771 8s. 2d.

Owing to press of work I have been unable fully to inquire into the expenditure in all the cases where I have recommended advances, this I hope to do during the present year.

GENERAL REMARKS.

I do not yet feel justified in giving any very pronounced opinion upon the question of loans, but that in some cases they have been productive of good, I think may be inferred from the great increase in the number of boats and men employed in the fisheries in one locality, since the Reproductive Loan Fund Act has been in force, viz., in the district of Ballydavid, west of Dingle, in the county Kerry.

In 1874 there were 26 yawls and canoes in this guard, in 1880 the number had increased to no less than 62, all registered boats.

In this locality a large number of loans has been made, and I am glad to be able to speak highly of the correct manner in which the advances have been repaid, there being only two cases in which arrears have taken place for a sum of a little over £5 during the five years.

I have no doubt, however, that loans may be made advantageously for the encouragement of the fisheries if more supervision than we can possibly give could be secured, but this can only be done by the employment under us, of responsible persons to supervise in the various localities.

Referring to the total amount of arrears, I have reason to believe that in some cases where instalments have been paid in consequence of legal proceedings, several have not yet been brought to the credit of the fund.

If all amounts received had been included, I am satisfied that the sum overdue would be very much less than that shown in the returns.

                                                        JOS. HAYES.

MR. BRADY'S REPORT FOR THE COUNTIES OF LEITRIM, SLIGO, MAYO, GALWAY, CLARE, LIMERICK, AND PART OF KERRY.

COUNTY LEITRIM.

In this county there were £349 available for 1879. Only two applications for loans received during the year amounting to £40, but I could not recommend either. Seaboard of this county very small, and in reality I could not count on more than one crew of bona fide fishermen in the county. The money for this county, which has been lying idle for many years, I should like to see transferred to other counties where it is so much required.

COUNTY SLIGO.

In this county there were £458 available for the year 1879. There were 47 applications received from 53 persons amounting to £887. 27 loans were recommended amounting to £380 in sums varying from £5 to £40. Out of this only £358 were issued the balance not having been taken up.

In many places in this county these loans have done good, but I have found great difficulty in enforcing the proper application of the money. The enforcement of this rule which is of such importance to the fishermen themselves, I think, has been one of the causes of checking the demand for loans in this county. By a return received from the Board of Works I find there were only the following instalments stated to be in arrear—

						£	s.	d.
In the cases of	6	of the loans made in	1875,	instalments amounting to	. .	21	2	8
„	1	„	1876,	„ „	. .	3	19	9
„	3	„	1877,	„ „	. .	14	10	0
„	3	„	1878,	„ „	. .	10	1	6 ·
						£49	13	11

Although I should like to be able to report much smaller arrears, yet I think it speaks creditably of the people that the amount is not larger. In most of the cases there is ample security for the repayment of the arrears, the great bulk of which is the instalments of some of these which fell due in 1879.

The total amount issued in this county for five years was £1,436, out of which there have been repaid £812 4s. 9d.

County Mayo.

The amount available for this county for 1879, was £670.

There were 144 applications received from 282 persons amounting to £2,020 9s., out of these there were 60 loans recommended, for the full amount available, viz.:—£670, all of which was issued.

Loans ranged from £5 to £30. So far as I was able to investigate the matter I think the loans in this county were generally fairly and well expended, and I know did a great deal of good. Many persons have declared to me that they could not have fished, and would have been obliged to abandon it, but for the loans they had received. In some cases I have heard most gratifying accounts of the results when industry and perseverance have been exercised. In one or two such cases I have heard that not only did the loans even of small amounts not exceeding £10, enable the parties to continue fishing, but having had a good take of fish they were enabled to purchase a new outfit of gear and boat, and to maintain themselves and their families, without charitable relief during a season which proved very hard on the poor.

The amount of money available for this county which has such an immense extent of seaboard is wholly insufficient for the absolutely necessary wants of the fishermen, and it can readily be understood with what difficulty the apportioning of a very small fund out of so many more *bond fide* equally good applications is surrounded. Nearly all the applications are investigated by me; and when this is done I make the best selection I can, but in doing so I am obliged, from want of funds, to reject many deserving cases.

There were 282 persons applied for loans, and out of which I could only recommend for the reasons given 111 persons. No matter how carefully or independently this duty may be performed it is an unenviable one, and cannot be discharged with satisfaction to either parties; as the feeling must remain of having rejected as good and deserving people as those selected.

I find by the return received from the Board of Works that the following instalments of loans were overdue up to March last—

							£	s.	d.
In the cases of	6 loans made in 1875, instalments amounting to			.	.		27	8	0
„	16	„	1876,	„	„	.	54	12	3
„	8	„	1877,	„	„	.	30	11	6
„	3	„	1878,	„	„	.	6	13	6
				Total,	.	.	£119	4	3

I cannot vouch for the accuracy of this return as several persons mentioned therein as still being in arrear, have stated to me when I remonstrated with them against being so that they had paid the instalments either to the Attorneys or the Sheriff's Officer with costs.

The total amount issued for this county during the five years was £3,306, and the repayments were £1,947 13s. 11d.

County Galway.

The sum available for the year 1879, was £1,141. There were 188 applications received from 394 persons amounting to £3,591. I was only able to recommend 82 loans amounting to £1,117 among 140 persons, in sums varying from £5 to £50. Out of this sum only £1,040 were issued, the balance not having been taken up. The same observations I have made in the case of the county Mayo, are applicable to this county. The amount is wholly insufficient to meet the wants of those who really deserve to receive loans, and many legitimate cases had in consequence to be rejected. I know of many instances in this county where fishing could not have been carried on in the absence of these loans.

By the return from the Board of Works the following appears to be the list of arrears—

							£	s.	d.
In the cases of	4 loans made in 1875, instalments are in arrears to amount of			.			10	5	11
„	10	„	1876,	„	„	„	.	39	6	6
„	8	„	1877,	„	„	„	.	15	14	6
„	4	„	1878,	„	„	„	.	10	14	1
				Total,		.	£66	1	0

The total amount issued for the five years in this county was £5,375 10s., and the repayments amounted to £3,529 5s. 11d.

County Limerick.

The sum available for this county was £625.

No applications were received. No *bond fide* sea fishermen in the county.

County Clare.

The amount available was £868. There were 33 applications received from 44 persons amounting to £523 10s. 24 loans were recommended to the amount of £361 among 30 persons. The amount available for this county is also wholly insufficient to meet the legitimate demands of the fishermen.

The observations I have felt it my duty to make in the cases of Galway and Mayo are equally applicable to this county.

A great deal of good has been done to the fishermen by means of these loans in this county, and many have been kept at it who would otherwise have not been able to fish—and I know myself of large captures of herrings and mackerel having been made by the nets and boats purchased by this money. The great bulk of fishing in this county is carried on by means of curraghs or canoes, and about £12 can fit out one of these with nets for three men who are enabled in the harvest time to make a good fishing of herrings and mackerel.

When the natural harbours of Goleen Moveen, at which the Board of Works are now at work, Goleen Ross, and Goleen Tullig are cleared of the rocks which have heretofore proved so fatal to these frail barks and which have caused such loss of life, I anticipate most important results in the production of a vastly increased supply of fish. In the season the mackerel are within pistol-shot of the shore of this iron-bound coast, but the canoes can seldom make more than one fishing of a night, as they have to catch the tide to get over or past the rocks in these harbours, whereas when they are cleared they may be able to load their canoes several times during the night and return in comparative safety.

I dwell on this matter, perhaps not in its proper place, in consequence of the number and amount of loans made in the locality which have proved so useful—but what they might have proved to be to the poor along this coast if they had a safe place to return to from the sea, few can tell. Not only would the fishermen be enabled to live and rear their families without having recourse to charity, but in a short time might be enabled to do altogether without the aid of loans—at any rate of this there cannot be the slightest doubt, that there would be an enormous increase in the supply of food.

By the return from the Board of Works the following appears to be the state of the arrear list :—

							£	s.	d.
In the cases of	5	loans made in	1875	instalments in arrears amounting to	.	.	6	2	1
„	7	„	1876	„	„	„	.	. 14 18	6
„	11	„	1877	„	„	„	.	. 30 0	0
„	4	„	1878	„	„	„	.	. 9 10	6
					Total,	.	£60 11	1	

With regard to the arrears in this county also there are several instalments included in the above as in arrear where the parties have assured me that they had paid them. And, indeed, in some cases I have seen with them the receipts for the debt and costs.

The total amount issued for this county for the 5 years was £1,681, and the repayments were £962 9s. 3d.

County Kerry.

From that part of the county under my charge there were 13 applications received from 17 persons amounting to £526 2s., and 7 loans to the amount of £310 recommended among 10 persons. Of this only £295 were issued, the balance not having been taken up. I have been wholly unable from the pressure of other business to investigate the expenditure of these loans, but hope to do so shortly.

General Remarks.

Every year's experience still further convinces me of the great importance of these loans to the poor fishermen. In my opinion their fishing pursuits are far more valuable than their farming, and both can be carried on together with great advantage not only to the people themselves who follow this pursuit as a part of their means of living but to the country at large by the production of a large quantity of valuable food.

Along the west coast there are few people who do not at some season or other of the year follow fishing of some description or other. The small patches of land they hold in most cases are wholly insufficient from which to support themselves or their families, but with the aid of fishing combined with their little farming they might be able to make out a tolerably comfortable existence. Without proper appliances for fishing they cannot follow fishing, and they are utterly unable to supply these wants themselves without the aid of loans. It is, therefore, I believe for the interests of the country that loans in such cases should not only be made, but be more extended than heretofore, and from the past I have every reason to think that in the great majority of cases they will be punctually repaid, and that the money as a rule will be fairly applied. My observations have reference particularly to the whole of the west coast where small loans of from £6 to £10 and £15 will prove and have proved of great benefit. I regret this fund is not applicable to the county of Donegal, the poor fishermen of which bear a remarkably good character for truth and honesty, and who are deserving of aid from the State in this way as much as any class of men round the whole coast that I know.

With regard to the amount of arrears returned by the Board of Works I cannot help saying that much of this arrear, *where it really does exist*, is caused by inactivity in enforcing payments. I know cases where the sureties for loans have been decreed, and where the sheriff's officer had only to walk into the place and levy for a far greater amount than that of the decree, without the slightest danger or fear of meeting difficulties or default of any description, and yet these decrees have been allowed to hang over without any steps being taken on them for months and months, and I might, I believe, say years.

We have repeatedly urged on the Board of Works the importance of causing returns to decrees to be made to them by the sheriffs or the attorneys in whose hands the amounts have been placed for collection. Several people now appearing on the list have satisfied me that they have paid the amounts with costs a long time ago. We brought this matter also under the notice of the Board, but they say that until the money is actually received by them the parties must still be returned as in arrear. This swells the amount of arrears, which I can hardly think is fair, towards the administrators of this fund, who have taken every precaution in their power to prevent bad debts being made. And so far as my district is concerned I am pretty confident that very few such would eventually be found if some better system of collection could be adopted.

It is right for me to say that we have nothing whatever to do with the issue of money or recovery of payments of instalments. The Board of Works alone are charged with this duty.

In concluding my observations on this subject I think it only due to the Coast Guard and Royal Irish Constabulary, to say that I have invariably received from them the most cordial and valuable assistance in administering this fund. In fact they have never thought any request I made either inconvenient or troublesome, but with a most cordial alacrity endeavoured on all occasions to meet my wishes and give me the fullest and most confidential information.

To those country gentlemen and others to whom I felt it necessary to apply for confidential information, and who have on many occasions given me important aid, my best thanks are also due.

THOMAS F. BRADY.

MR. JOHNSTON'S REPORT.

DIVISION extends from WICKLOW HEAD to MULLAGHMORE, County SLIGO, embracing in whole or part the Counties of WICKLOW, DUBLIN, KILDARE, KING'S COUNTY, MEATH, WESTMEATH, LOUTH, CAVAN, LONGFORD, MONAGHAN, DOWN, ARMAGH, ANTRIM, LONDONDERRY, FERMANAGH, TYRONE, DONEGAL, LEITRIM, and SLIGO, and including the eight DISTRICTS of DUBLIN, DROGHEDA, DUNDALK, BALLYCASTLE, COLERAINE, LONDONDERRY, LETTERKENNY, and BALLYSHANNON.

No. 1, or DUBLIN DISTRICT

Extends from Wicklow Head to Skerries, county Dublin, embracing in part or whole the counties of Wicklow, Dublin, Kildare, and Meath.

Close Seasons.

Tidal Waters—From Howth to Dalkey Island—Between 15th August and 1st of February. For remainder of district—Between 15th September and 2nd March.
Fresh Water—Same. Angling with cross lines—Same. Angling with single rod and line—Between 31st October and 1st February.

Bye-Laws.—River Liffey.

Prohibiting the catching, or attempting to catch, salmon with any net of greater length than 350 yards between Island-bridge weir and a line drawn due north from Poolbeg Lighthouse.
Permitting the use of nets with meshes of one inch from knot to knot for the capture of salmon or trout between Dalkey Island and Wicklow Head.

Report.

The general state of the salmon fisheries in this district, during 1879, has been prosperous.
There has been a slight falling off in the number of engines used in this district, as compared with 1878, in which year there were in use 97 salmon rods, 1 cross line, and 16 draft nets. In 1879 the numbers were, 89 salmon rods, 2 cross lines, and 18 draft nets.
The receipts were nearly the same as in 1878. The amount taken for salmon rods was £89; for cross lines, £4; for draft nets, £54; making, with £3 16s. 8d. for fines, a total of £150 16s. 8d., as compared with £131 4s. 10d. in 1878.
The average weight of salmon taken was 9 lbs.; that of peale, 4 lbs.
The highest price given for salmon was 2s. 8d.; the lowest, 1s. 2d. per lb.
The take of salmon and grilse in this district was about the same as in 1878.
There are no water-bailiffs employed by the Board; but the Conservators allow the Swords Angling Club £10 per annum towards the protection of the Swords River. The Clerk of the Conservators acts as inspector of the district.
There are five water-bailiffs employed by private individuals—two by the Earl of Meath, on the Bray River; one by Mr. R. Cane, of St. Wolstan's; and two by the Swords Angling Club.
There were two successful prosecutions by the Constabulary during the year for breaches of the fishery laws. The greater portion of the upper waters of the district is protected by the proprietors, who do not permit trespass on the lands adjoining.

No. 13, or BALLYSHANNON DISTRICT

Extends from Rossan Point, county Donegal, to Mullaghmore, county Sligo.

Close Seasons.

For Tidal and Fresh Waters—Between 19th August and 1st March, save River Eske and tributaries, which is 17th September and 1st April.
For angling with Single Rods—Between 9th October and 1st March, save Bunduff, which is between 30th September and 1st February; Bundrowes, between 30th September and 1st January, and, save Erne, between 30th September and 1st March.

D

Bye-Laws.

Permitting use of nets, with meshes of 1 inch from knot to knot, in tideway of River Erne.

Repealing bye-law of 24th February, 1860, prohibiting use of nets with meshes less than 1 inch for capture of fish of any kind on that part of the coast of the county Donegal inside or to the north-east and north of lines drawn from Rossan Point to Teelin Head, and from Teelin Head to Carrigan Head, and from Carrigan Head to Muckross Point, all in the barony of Bannagh, and county of Donegal.

Permitting use of nets with meshes of 1 inch from knot to knot, for capture of fish by persons having right to use nets in Lough Erne, between Enniskillen and Belleek, between 1st May and 1st day of close season in each year.

Prohibiting the capture of fish of any description with the instrument commonly called and known by the name of the Spoonbait, or any other instrument of the like nature or device, during the months of January, February, and March in each year, in that part of the River Erne situated between the Falls of Belleek and a line drawn due south across the river, from the point of Castlecaldwell Demesne, by the eastern point of the Muckinish, or White Island, to the opposite bank, all in the county of Fermanagh.

Permitting use of nets for the capture of fish with meshes of 1 inch from knot to knot (to be measured along the side of the square, or 4 inches to be measured all round each such mesh, such measurements being taken in the clear when the net is wet), within so much of the River Eany Water, or Inver, in the county of Donegal, as lies above the mouth of said river as defined.

Report.

The general state of the salmon fisheries in this district, during 1879, was fair; though, except in the River Erne, the take of salmon and grilse was less than in 1878.

The receipts for 1879 were, for salmon rods, £113; cross lines and rods, £12; draft nets, £138; pole nets, £2; stake weirs, £30; box, cribs, &c., £40; eel nets, £35; pollen nets, £1 10s.; from fines, £4 15s. 2d.; interest on bank account, £2 10s. 4d.; subscriptions received, £5 9s. 10d.; making a total of £384 5s. 4d., as against £370 18s. 8d. in 1879.

The engines used were 113 salmon rods, 6 cross lines, 46 draft nets, 1 pole net, 1 stake net, 4 boxes or cribs, and 35 gaps or eyes for eels.

The average weight of salmon taken was 13 lbs.; of peale, 6¼ lbs. The highest price given for salmon was 2s. 6d.; the lowest, 10d. per lb.

About the same quantity of breeding fish was observed in the district as in 1878.

Nine prosecutions were instituted by the Conservators, of which 5 were successful. About 200 water bailiffs are employed by the Conservators. The Marquis of Ely, Mr. William Sinclair, and Mr. Musgrave also employ water bailiffs.

No. 14, or LETTERKENNY DISTRICT

Extends from Malin Head to Rossan Point, county Donegal, and comprises the greater part of the county Donegal.

Close Seasons.

Tidal Water—Between 19th August and 4th February, and one mile above tideway, save Crana or Buncrana and Gweebarra Rivers. For Crana or Buncrana—Between 14th September and 15th April. For Gweebarra—Between 30th September and 1st April.

Fresh Water—Between 19th August and 1st March, save Crana or Buncrana River, Leenane and Gweeharra Rivers, which are the same as tidal. Angling with cross lines—Same as netting in fresh water. Angling with single rod and line—Between 1st November and 1st February; save in Buncrana. Crana or Buncrana—Between 31st October and 1st March.

Bye-Law.

Permitting the use of nets for the capture of salmon or trout, with meshes of one inch from knot to knot, in the Crana or Buncrana river, and within one mile seawards and coastwards thereof.

Report.

The general state of the salmon fisheries, in this district, was good.

Except in draft nets, which were 6, in 1879, as compared with 13, in 1878, and of loop nets, 15, in 1879, and 6 in 1878, the number of engines used was about the same as in 1878.

The receipts were, for salmon rods, £43 ; for draft nets, £48 ; for drift nets, £18 ; bag nets, £30 ; box, £10 ; loop nets, £15. The fines amounted to £9 17s. 8d. ; sale of forfeited engines, 6s. ; rates on Poor Law valuation of several fisheries, £14. The total amount of receipts was £188 3s. 8d. (not including £2 15s., interest on balance in Bank) as against £196 18s. 5d. in 1878.

The average weight of salmon taken was 10 lbs. ; of peale 6 lbs. The highest price given was 2s. ; the lowest, 6d. per lb.

The take of salmon and grilse, in the district, was much less than in 1878.

The quantity of breeding fish, however, has been much greater this year.

Three water-bailiffs are employed by the Conservators, and 121, during the close season, and 103, the rest of the year, by the Marquis of Conyngham, Lord Cloncurry, Lord Leitrim, Sir J. Stewart, and Messrs. Stewart, Olpherts, Richardson, and Lingard.

The number of prosecutions instituted by the Conservators, in 1879, was 13, out of which there were 9 convictions ; five of the prosecutions were at the instance of the Constabulary.

Offences against the fishery laws are reported as having decreased, though the number of prosecutions was slightly in excess of these in 1878.

No. 15¹, LONDONDERRY DISTRICT

Extends from Downhill boundary, county Derry, to Malin Head, county Donegal, includes parts of Derry, Donegal, and Tyrone.

Close Seasons.

Tidal—Between 31st August and 15th April.
Fresh Water—Same. Angling with cross lines—28th September and 15th April. Angling with single rod—Between 1st November and 1st February.

Bye-Laws.

Permitting the use of nets for capture of fish other than salmon and trout with meshes of half an inch from knot to knot in Baronscourt Lakes and Streams.

Permitting the use of nets with meshes of one inch from knot to knot in Lough Foyle and tidal parts of the river.

Prohibiting having nets for the capture of salmon or trout in or on board any boat, cot, or curragh, in the tidal waters of said district, which comprises the whole of the sea along the coast between Malin Head, in the county of Donegal, and the townland boundary between the townlands of Drumagully and Downhill, in the county of Londonderry, with the whole of the tideway along said coast and rivers, and the whole of the tidal portion of the several rivers and their tributaries flowing into said coast between said points at any time *between the hours of Twelve of the Clock at noon on Saturday, and Four of the Clock on Monday Morning.*

Report.

The general state of the salmon fisheries, in this district, has not been so satisfactory as for the past few years.

There has been a considerable increase in the number of engines used, in this district. The number in use in 1879 was—88 salmon rods, 7 cross lines, 33 draft nets, 45 drift nets, 3 pole nets, 4 bag nets, and 3 stake nets.

The receipts were, for salmon rods, £88 ; cross lines, £14 ; draft nets, £99 ; drift nets, £135 ; pole nets, £6 ; bag nets, £40 ; stake nets, £90 ; with £13 3s. 9d. for fines ; amount of rates on Poor Law valuation on several fisheries, £95 ; subscriptions from lessees of the Irish Society, £605 ; making a total of £1,185 3s. 9d., as against £1,197 18s. 8d. in 1878.

The average weight of salmon taken was 11 lbs. ; of peale, 6 lbs. The highest price given for salmon was 1s 6d. ; the lowest, 8d. per lb.

The take of salmon and grilse in the district was considerably less in 1879 than in 1878. Young fish appeared earlier in 1879 than formerly, on account of the large quantity of water coming from the rivers.

The quantity of breeding fish observed was greater than in 1878.

Much destruction of fry, during their descent to the sea, takes place, especially by unlicensed anglers fishing for trout.

Two hundred and thirty water-bailiffs are employed by the Conservators for about four months, and a few of those are retained during the year.

Eight successful prosecutions were instituted by the Conservators, and six by the Constabulary.

No. 15², or COLERAINE DISTRICT

Extends from Portrush, county Antrim, to Downhill boundary, county Derry, embracing parts of the counties Monaghan, Armagh, Down, Antrim, and Derry.

Close Seasons.

Tidal portion—Between 19th August and 4th February.

Fresh water—Between 19th August and 1st March. Angling with single rods—Between 19th October and 16th March, save Bann and its tributaries. For Bann and its tributaries—Between 31st October and 1st March. Cross lines—28th September and 16th March. Pollen fishing by trammel nets in Lough Neagh—Between 19th August and 1st March.

Bye-Laws.

Prohibiting the use of draft nets for the capture of pollen in Lough Neagh.

Permitting pollen to be taken by trammel or set nets, composed of yarn of a fine texture, not less than ten hanks to the pound weight, doubled and twisted with a mesh of not less than one inch from knot to knot, between 1st February and 31st October, in Lough Neagh.

Prohibiting the snatching, or attempting to snatch, salmon in any of the tidal or fresh waters of district.

Prohibiting the having any net for the capture of salmon or trout, in or on board any boat, cot, or curragh, in the tidal waters of said district, which comprises the tidal portions of all rivers and their tributaries flowing into the sea along the coast between the sea-point of the townland boundary between the townlands of Downhill and Drumagully, in the county of Londonderry, and the point of Portrush, in the county of Antrim, at any time between the hours of 12 o'clock at noon on Saturday and 4 o'clock on Monday morning.

Prohibiting the having any net for the capture of salmon, trout, or pollen in or on board any boat, cot, or curragh, in Lough Neagh or Lough Beg, situated within the aforesaid district, at any time between the hours of 11 o'clock in the forenoon on Saturday and 4 o'clock on Monday morning.

Report.

The general state of the salmon fisheries in this district, during 1879, showed a considerable improvement.

There was a large increase in the number of engines used in the district, over 1878, in salmon rods, trammel nets, and eel nets. There were in use, in 1879, 110 salmon rods, 129 draft nets, 135 trammel nets, 2 bag nets, 4 boxes, and 64 eel nets.

The receipts, in 1879, were, for salmon rods, £110 ; draft nets, £387 ; trammel nets, £135 ; bag nets, £20 ; boxes, £40 ; eel nets, £192 ; fines, £119 15s. 3d. ; salmon forfeited, 14s. ; rates on Poor Law valuation of several fisheries, £96 ; making a total of £1,100 9s. 3d., as compared with £1,179 6s. 9d. in 1878.

The average weight of salmon taken was about 10 lbs.

The highest price given for salmon was 2s. 6d. ; the lowest, 10d. per lb.

The take of salmon was rather less in 1879 than in 1878, in consequence of the great floods. From the same cause a considerable number of fish appeared in the rivers a month earlier than usual.

The quantity of breeding fish observed in the rivers was considerably greater than in 1878.

Sixty-two water-bailiffs and five inspectors are employed for the whole year by the Conservators, and two water-bailiffs by Mr. S. M. Alexander.

The number of prosecutions by the Conservators was 105; those undertaken by the Constabulary were 12.

No. 16¹, or BALLYCASTLE DISTRICT

Extends from Donaghadee, county Down, to Portrush, county Antrim, containing portions of the counties of Down, Antrim, and Derry.

Close Seasons.

Tidal—Between 19th August and 4th February.
Fresh Water—19th August and 1st March. Cross lines—28th September and 16th March. Single rod and line—1st November and 1st February.
Engines used in 1877—25 salmon rods, 12 draft nets, and 14 bag nets.

Bye-Laws—Bush River.

Repealing definition of Bush River Estuary, as fixed by late Special Commissioners on 8th February, 1864.

Report.

The general state of the salmon fisheries, in this district, during 1879, was not satisfactory.

There were in use, in 1879, 28 salmon rods, 9 draft nets, and 14 bag nets, as compared with 22 salmon rods, 11 draft nets, and 14 bag nets, in 1878.

The receipts were, for salmon rods, £22; for draft nets, £27; and for bag nets, £140; making, with £19 1s. 1d. fines, and £53, rates on Poor Law Valuation of several fisheries, a total of £261 1s. 1d., as compared with £237 11s. 3d., in 1878. A sum of £185 6s. 9d. has been expended by the proprietors, in the protection of their fisheries, over and above the receipts of the Board.

The average weight of salmon taken was about 8 lbs. The highest price given was 2s.; the lowest 8d. per lb.

The quantity of breeding fish observed was about the same as in 1878.

Upwards of forty water-bailiffs are employed by private individuals, during the close season, viz., by Earl of Antrim, Sir F. E. MacNaghten, bart., Sir F. Boyd, bart., and Mr. John Finlay.

There were six successful prosecutions by the Constabulary during the year. Offences against the fishery laws have considerably diminished in this district.

No. 17¹, or DROGHEDA DISTRICT

Extends from Skerries, county Dublin, to Clogher Head, county Louth, and embraces portions of the counties of Dublin, Louth, King's County, Meath, Westmeath, and Cavan.

Close Seasons.

For all Engines—Between 4th August and 12th February.

No Bye-Laws.

Report.

The general state of the salmon fisheries in this district, during the year 1879, has been satisfactory.

The number of engines used in the district was, in 1878, 66 salmon rods, 5 cross lines, 6 snap nets, 61 draft nets, 5 boxes, and 44 eel nets; in 1879, 60 salmon rods, 5 cross lines, 4 snap nets, 66 draft nets, 4 boxes, and 38 eel nets.

The receipts were, for salmon rods, £60; for cross lines, £10; for snap nets, £6; for draft nets, £198; for boxes, £40; and for eel nets, £38; making, with £8 14s. 9d. for fines, £1 3s. 4d. for forfeited engines, and £2 subscriptions, a total of £363 18s. 1d., as compared with £363 6s. 8d. in 1878.

The average weight of salmon taken was 16 lbs.; of peale, 5 lbs.

The highest price given for salmon was 2s. 4d.; the lowest, 1s. per lb.

The take of salmon during the season has been very variable; but, on the whole, has been a fair average.

Breeding fish have gone up in large numbers, and the spawning beds are fully occupied.

Ten water-bailiffs are employed by the Conservators, and two by the Marquis of Headford, Mr. J. L. W. Naper, and others conjointly.

There was only one case of successful prosecution by the Conservators, and four by the Constabulary.

No. 17, or DUNDALK DISTRICT

Extends from Clogher Head, county Louth, to Donaghadee, county Down, embracing, in whole or part, the counties of Louth, Meath, Down, Armagh, Monaghan, and Cavan.

Close Seasons.

For tidal and fresh waters, save in Annagassan, Glyde, Dee, Fane, and their tributaries—Between 31st August and 1st April. In Glyde, Dee, and Annagassan—Between 19th August and 12th February. Fane River—Between 19th August and 1st April.

Angling with cross lines—Same as netting. Angling with single rod—11th October to 1st of March, save in Annagassan, Glyde, and Dee. In Annagassan, Glyde, and Dee—Between 30th September and 1st of February.

Bye-Laws.

Prohibiting to catch, or attempting to catch, salmon or trout with any net of greater length than 500 yards between Clogher Head and Ballagan Point, county Louth.

Prohibiting to catch, or attempting to catch, salmon in any tidal water between Dunany Point and Soldiers' Point, county Louth, with a spear, lyster, otter, strokehaul, dree-draw, or gaff, except when the latter is used as an auxiliary with rod and line, or for removing fish from any legal weir or box by the owner or occupier thereof.

Report.

The general state of the salmon fisheries in this district, during 1879, was very good.

There has been a slight falling off in the number of engines used in the district, as compared with 1878; the number in 1879 being 48 salmon rods (three more than in any other year since the district was formed), 22 draft nets, 2 bag nets, 1 head weir, and 15 eel nets.

The receipts have, consequently, somewhat fallen off. They were, for salmon rods, £48; for draft nets, £66; for bag nets, £20; for a head weir, £6; for eel nets, £15.

The amount received from fines was £46 16s.; rates on Poor Law valuation of several fisheries, £11; subscriptions received, £3. The total receipts amounted to £215 16s., as compared with £239 5s. 6d. in 1879.

The average weight of salmon taken was 16 lbs.; of peale, 9 lbs.

The take of salmon and grilse in the district was much more productive than in 1878, which year showed an increase over 1877.

The highest price given for salmon was 2s. per lb.; the lowest, 9d.

The quantity of breeding fish continues to increase in the rivers; it was much greater in 1879 than in 1878.

The highest number of water-bailiffs employed was 9, and the lowest 6. An inspector of water-bailiffs is employed for 9 months.

Nine successful prosecutions were instituted by the Conservators.

Fifty successful prosecutions were instituted by the Constabulary. By far the larger number of these were for pollution of rivers by flax-water. Nearly all those latter were in the Ballynahinch locality intended to be embraced in the proposed Down district.

Concluding Remarks.

I have to express my regret that the necessary steps for the formation of the Down district have not yet been taken, owing to the inadequate support given to the preliminary expenses. I hope that proprietors and anglers, in Downshire, will come forward liberally, during the season, in order to have a project so desirable for the promotion of the fisheries duly carried out.

WILLIAM JOHNSTON.

MAJOR HAYES' REPORT.

Division extending from SLEA HEAD in the County of KERRY in the west to WICKLOW HEAD in the east, and including eight fishery districts—viz., No. 7, KILLARNEY; No. 6², KENMARE; No. 6², BANTRY; No. 6¹, SKIBBEREEN; No. 5, CORK; No. 4, LISMORE; No. 3, WATERFORD; and No. 2, WEXFORD, which embrace the whole or portions of the following counties, viz.:—KERRY, CORK, WATERFORD, TIPPERARY, LIMERICK, KILKENNY, CARLOW, WEXFORD, QUEEN'S COUNTY, KING'S COUNTY, KILDARE, and WICKLOW.

No. 7. KILLARNEY DISTRICT.

Extending from Lamb Head to Dunmore Head, both in the county of Kerry.

It is reported that the capture of salmon and trout in this district in 1879 slightly exceeded that for 1878; but on the whole in consequence of continuous floods during part of the season, it could not be considered altogether satisfactory.

The spawning beds have been well stocked.

Average weight of salmon,	.	.	12 lbs.
„ peale,	.	.	6 lbs.

Although it is reported that offences against the Fishery Laws have diminished, yet there were two cases of poisoning during the year in the Brown Flesk River.

There were 18 prosecutions, at the instance of the Board of Conservators, of these 16 were convicted, and in two cases only were the parties acquitted.

There were 81 water-bailiffs employed by the Board, and about 40 by private individuals. These numbers appear large, but considering the great extent of valuable spawning ground, it is quite insufficient to secure efficient protection, so much so, indeed, that one of the most important spawning rivers in the district—the Flesk—with its tributories receive, I may say, no protection whatever, and are systematically poached.

The Table of close seasons and the Bye-laws in force will be found at pp. 57, 60 and 61.

The following engines were licensed in 1879 for the capture of salmon and trout:—99 salmon rods, 5 cross lines, 52 draft nets, 2 boxes or cribs, producing with fines and the amount received under the Poor Law Valuation a total of £333 9s. available for protection, being less by £69 12s. than the amount received for 1878.

With the exception of this very important point—viz. "insufficiency of funds" to ensure efficient protection—I consider the condition of the fisheries of this district to be satisfactory.

No 6². KENMARE DISTRICT.

Extending from Crow Head to Lamb Head, Co. Kerry.

The capture of salmon is reported to have been less than in the preceding year.

The Bye-law alluded to in our last report limiting the size of the nets to be used in this district, and prohibiting the practice of throwing stones and beating the water during the shooting or drafting of such nets has since received approval and has become law.

The spawning beds have been satisfactorily stocked—in the River Sheen the stock was much greater than in 1878.

Offences against the Fishery Laws are reported to have diminished; but there have been several cases of poisoning in the Roughty river.

Indeed, the only offences for which prosecutions are reported to have taken place, were for taking or attempting to take poisoned fish. There were 13 persons prosecuted for this offence; of these 5 only were convicted.

It may be well to mention that fish poisoned by "lime" or "spurge" are not considered by the country people unfit for food.

The engines for capture of salmon and trout in this district in 1879 were 26 single rods, 5 draft nets or seines, 1 bag net, and 4 sweepers. The amount realized for protection from these together with the 10 per cent. in Poor Law Valuation of Fisheries, &c., amounted to £70 5s. 10d., as compared with £63 10s. for 1878.

For Table of close seasons, see pp. 57, 60 and 61.

Artificial propagation is still very successfully carried on by Richard Mabony, esq., of Dromore Castle, he having turned out no less than about 120,000 healthy young salmon into the Blackwater last year; and in the process of hatching it is believed that the loss did not exceed one per cent.

No. 6². Bantry District.

Extending from Mizen Head to Crow Head, in the county of Cork.

It is reported that in consequence of the continuous floods, the netting season was most unproductive, whilst the rod fishing was very good.

The quantity of breeding fish on the spawning beds, was reported as "never greater."

There were no prosecutions for offences against the Fishery Laws, although it is stated that the Durrus river was poisoned three times.

The Bye-laws, referring to this district and the tables of close seasons will be found at pp. 57, 60 and 61.

Licensed engines during 1879—9 single rods, 10 draft nets.

The total amount received and available for protection was £39 12s. 3d., being less by £8 7s. 9d. than that received in 1878.

No. 6¹. Skibbereen District.

Extending from Galley Head to Mizen Head, in the county of Cork.

Again I have to report unfavourably of the fisheries of this district.

It is difficult to ascertain the cause of the falling off in production. By some it is believed that the extension of the mackerel fishing off the coast, and the immense extent of the nets, has had something to do with it, by interrupting the run of salmon to the rivers; by others that the Bye-law permitting nets with meshes of one inch from knot to knot to be used, was the cause.

The latter is now, however, removed, as the repeal of this Bye-law received the sanction of the Lord Lieutenant and Privy Council on the 13th December last, and the Bye-law prohibiting the use of drift nets, has been also approved and is now in force.

The quantity of spawning fish in the river has been reported as rather less than in 1878.

No change is reported as to the size of the fish.

For Bye-laws and close season table see pages 57, 60 and 61 of Appendix.

Although poaching prevails to a considerable extent, the only prosecution instituted during the year was for flax steeping.

The following engines were duly licensed for taking salmon and trout in 1879—8 single rods and 15 draft nets. These, with £1 11s. 8d. received for fines, produced a sum of £45 11s. 8d. available for protection, as against £58 14s. received in 1878.

No. 5. Cork District.

Extending from Ballycotton Head to Galley Head, both in the county of Cork.

In the year 1879 the capture of fish was again most satisfactory, the quantity taken being in excess of that captured in 1878, in which year the capture was much greater than in the one preceding.

Although the Bye-laws, prohibiting the use of drift nets in the River Lee and estuary, have been found of great value, still it is almost impossible, with the limited means of protection available, to prevent their use, and there is no doubt but that much poaching with this engine was carried on during the year.

The stock of fish in the spawning grounds is reported as not so great as in 1878.

Rod fishings have enormously increased in value within the last few years, a most satisfactory proof that the district is prospering.

No change is reported as to the average size of salmon and peale.

Offences against the Fishery Laws are reported to have increased, although less prosecutions have taken place, there having been only 34 during the year, whereas in 1878 there were 51. Of the 34, 23 were convicted and 11 acquitted.

The Bye-law, prohibiting all netting for salmon and trout in certain parts of the Bandon River, has been renewed for a further period of five years from the 29th October last.

We have received an application to prohibit the use of nets for sea fish in certain parts of the tideway, as it is believed that this netting which is carried on ostensibly for sea fish, is in reality to a great extent for the capture of salmon.

This application will be the subject of a public inquiry.

A gun boat was stationed in the River Lee during a part of the close season for the purpose of aiding in the suppression of illegal fishing.

For close season tables and the Bye-laws in force, see pp. 56, 57, 60 and 61.

The following engines were licensed and fished during the year 1879—270 single rods, 2 cross lines, 70 draft nets, 9 drift nets, 1 bag net, and 1 stroke weir. These produced

£551, added to this £32 7s. for fines, £3 10s., amount received for sale of forfeited engines, and a contribution from the Cork Anglers' Club of £52 10s. and £2 interest from the bank—amounted on the whole, to £639 9s. 6d. available for protection.

The fisheries of the Cork district have improved steadily for several years.

The Conservators have done all in their power to secure this result, and they have been much assisted by the exertions of the Cork Anglers' Club. It is rumoured that the Club will soon cease to exist. This will be much to be deplored. Proprietors of fisheries and all others at all interested should use their best exertions to prevent it. If they do not it is feared they will have cause seriously for regret.

No. 4. LISMORE DISTRICT.

Extending from Ballycotton, in the county of Cork, to Helvick Head, in the county of Waterford.

The capture of salmon is reported to have increased in 1879, and the results have been very satisfactory.

The quantity of breeding fish in the spawning beds is reported also to have been greater than in the year 1878.

Less offences against the Fishery Laws are reported as having taken place, although the number of prosecutions was greater than in 1878. Of these 33 were at the instance of the Constabulary, 22 by the Coast Guards, and 66 by the water-bailiffs.

For close season tables and the Bye-laws in force, see pp. 56, 60 and 61.

The following engines were duly licensed in 1879 :—259 single rods, 9 cross lines, 34 snap nets, 10 draft nets, 97 drift nets, 1 pole net, 2 stake nets, and 2 boxes or cribs, these produced £741. In addition to this £36 13s. 3d. was received for fines, £9 5s. 8d. sale of forfeited engines, £24 16s. Poor Law Valuation on Fisheries, and £24 10s. subscriptions. The whole available for protection amounting to £836 4s. 11d.

No. 5, or WATERFORD DISTRICT.

Extending from Helvick Head, in the county of Waterford, to Kiln Bay (East of Bannon Bay), in the county of Wexford.

The reports from this district as regards the capture of salmon and the stock of breeding fish on the spawning beds are most satisfactory, the capture considerably exceeding that for 1878, and the number of breeding fish greater.

The average size of salmon and peale about the same as in 1878.

Repeated statements had been from time to time made that the netting as carried on between Carrick and Waterford by seine nets was not satisfactory, and in July we received a memorial signed by three of the Conservators and a larger number of cot or snap net fishermen praying for an inquiry.

In consequence we held public inquiry into the subject at Waterford and Carrick on the 23rd and 25th August respectively.

It appeared from the evidence that the seine nets used were about 80 yards in length, there was nothing shown, however, to induce us to consider it necessary to prohibit their use. But it was clearly shown that fishing was practiced in January and February in these reaches of the river before the season opened, and that literally there was scarcely any attempt at preservation on the part of the Board of Conservators.

It occurred to us that it might be advisable to prohibit all kinds of netting within certain limits during the month of February, and in consequence we issued the following notice :—

"The Inspectors of Irish Fisheries hereby give notice that they propose to make a bye-law to prohibit the use of nets of any description in that part of the River Suir situated between the Bridge of Waterford and Fiddown-bridge, in the counties of Waterford and Kilkenny, during the month of February in any year, but before doing so they will be prepared to receive and consider any objections that may be made in writing from any person interested in the fisheries of such river, before the 1st day of November, 1879."

We have since received memorials praying that the Bye-law may not be made, and as yet we have not decided what course will be most advantageous to the fisheries to adopt.

In consequence of applications for a change of season for River Suir and tributaries, we also held inquiry into the subject on the 22nd, 27th and 29th August at Waterford, Clonmel, and Cahir respectively, and after receiving very full evidence on the subject decided to make certain changes which came into force in October last

The old close season order fixed the close season for nets and all other engines except single rods and lines from 15th August to 1st February. For single rods and lines 30th September to 1st February.

E

The new close season order which is now in force, fixes the close season for all engines same as the old, except as regards single rods and lines, which is now from 15th September to 1st February.

It was clearly shown that most of the fish captured by rods between 15th and 30th September were gravid and almost ready to spawn.

I feel bound to remark that great laxity appears to have prevailed with the Board of Conservators and their officers, in not making sufficient efforts to secure a proper observance of the law in the waters between Carrick and Waterford. I trust now that particular attention has been directed to the subject, means may be taken to secure this for the future.

It is almost impossible to say with certainty whether or not offences against the Fishery Laws have increased or diminished; in some places it is believed they have decreased.

During the year, there were 73 prosecutions; of these 45 were by the Constabulary, and 29 by the Board of Conservators; of the former 36 were convicted and fined, and 9 acquitted; of the latter 21 were convicted and 8 acquitted.

Having received an application to re-define the boundary of the mouth or estuary of the River Bannow, county Wexford, we held a public inquiry into the subject at Duncormack in June last year, and we decided to change the mouth as originally defined—it is now placed about a mile below Wellington Bridge, as shown on map or plan attached to the definition—this only received approval on 24th February last, and will appear fully in Report for 1880.

The following engines for the capture of salmon and trout were licensed in 1879.

224 single rods; 11 cross lines; 241 snap nets; 32 draft nets; 61 seines; 4 stake weirs; 4 boxes or cribs; and 25 gaps, eyes, or baskets for eels. The foregoing produced a sum of £1,071 10s., added to which £56 3s. 1d. for fines—£2 7s. produce of sales of forfeited engines—£6 2s. 8d., interest on deposit receipts, would show a total of £1,286 2s. 9d. available for protection.

For bye-laws and close season table see pages 56, 60 and 61 of Appendix.

No. 2.—WEXFORD DISTRICT.

Extending from Wicklow Head in the County of Wicklow to Kiln Bay (east of Bannow Bay), in the County of Wexford.

The Reports from this district are most satisfactory, and the capture of salmon was much in excess of that taken in 1878.

The spawning grounds are reported to have been fully stocked.

The average weight of salmon is stated to have been 14 lb., peale 5 lb.

Offences against the Fishery Laws diminished.

Twenty-seven persons were prosecuted for breaches of the Fishery Laws; of these 17 were convicted and 10 acquitted.

The Conservators have applied to us to prevent by bye-law, boats having nets on board during the annual close season above Ferrycarrig Bridge, as it is alleged that great poaching prevails there, and that in reality, although they are ostensibly for sea fishing, they are used for taking salmon only.

This application will if possible be the subject of inquiry during the present summer.

For close season tables and bye-laws in force in the district, see pp. 56, 60 and 61 of Appendix.

The following engines were duly licensed in 1879, for the capture of salmon, 86 single rods, 55 draft nets, and 1 pole net—The license duty amounted to £232, which with £50 5s. 6d. received for fines, amounted to £302 5s. 6d. available for protection.

CONCLUDING OBSERVATIONS.

Although throughout Ireland, the season of 1879 was under the average, yet, it is satisfactory to find that in some districts the capture was considerably in excess of previous years—and on the whole the south of Ireland contributed a large proportion to the gross capture—the following districts were exceedingly prosperous, viz., Cork, Lismore, Waterford, and Wexford.

I can but reiterate what I have stated in former reports upon the laxity prevailing with Boards of Conservators, generally, in not taking proper steps to secure equitable valuation of the several proprietory fisheries in their respective districts. The neglect is inexcusable, as if properly looked after, a large addition to the funds for protection would be secured annually which could be well employed, and is so much needed.

The Royal Irish Constabulary and the Coast Guards have during 1879, rendered most valuable aid in securing the observance of the Fishery Laws.

The salmon fisheries in the portion of Ireland under my superintendence, I consider generally to be in a very satisfactory condition.

JOS. HAYES.

MR. BRADY'S REPORT

ON DIVISION OF IRELAND extending from DUNMORE HEAD, in the county of Kerry, to MULLAGHMORE, in the county of Sligo, embracing in whole or part the counties of Kerry, Clare, Limerick, Tipperary, King's, Queen's, Galway, Longford, Westmeath, Roscommon, Leitrim, Mayo, Cavan, and Sligo.

No. 8, or LIMERICK DISTRICT,

Extends from Dunmore Head, in the county of Kerry, to Hag's Head, in the county of Clare, and includes all that part of the country the waters of which flow into the sea coast between those points.

Close Seasons.

The close seasons in this district are—For tidal and fresh waters :—

" Between 31st July and 12th February, save rivers Cashen and Tributaries, and save between Kerry Head and Dunmore Head, and Loop Head and Hag's Head, and all rivers running into the sea between those points.

" For Cashen down to its mouth and Tributaries, between 31st August and 1st June; between Dunmore Head and Kerry Head, and all rivers flowing into the sea between those points, between 15th September and 1st April ; between Loop Head and Hag's Head, and all rivers running into the sea between those points, between 15th September and 1st May."

For angling with single rods and lines :—

" Between 30th September and 1st February, save Feale, Geale, Cashen, Maigue and Mulkear, or Mulcair rivers, and their Tributaries ; and save all rivers running into the sea between Loop Head and Hag's Head, and between Dunmore Head and Kerry Head. For Feale, Geale, Cashen and Tributaries, between 31st October and 16th March; for Maigue and Tributaries, between 30th September and 20th February. For Mulkear or Mulcair and Tributaries, between 1st November and 31st January; between Loop Head and Hag's Head, between 30th September and 1st March, and between Dunmore Head and Kerry Head, between 30th September and 1st April."

Bye-laws.

The bye-laws in force in the district are as follows :—

In RIVER SHANNON :—

" Prohibiting net-fishing in that part of the River Shannon between Wellesley-bridge and the Railway bridge, between 1st June and 12th February.

" Prohibiting between the 1st day of August, or such other day as may be the first day of the close season, and the 1st day of November in each year, the use of draft nets, or any other net or nets used as a draft net, having a foot-rope and leads or weights affixed thereto, within the following limits, viz. :—In that part of the River Shannon situate between the Fishing weir known as the Lax Weir, and a line drawn due north and south across the said River Shannon at the western extremity of Graigue Island.

" Prohibiting draft nets for the capture of fish of any kind, of a mesh less than one and three-quarter inches from knot to knot, to be measured along the side of the square, or seven inches to be measured all round each such mesh, such measurements being taken in the clear when the net is wet, in the tidal parts of the River Shannon, or in the tidal parts of any rivers flowing into the said River Shannon.

" Prohibiting the fishing for salmon or trout by any means whatsoever, within a space of twenty yards from the weir wall of Tarmonbarry, on the River Shannon.

" Prohibiting having nets for capture of salmon or trout on board any cot or curragh between mouth of Shannon and Wellesley-bridge, in the city of Limerick, or in tidal parts of any rivers flowing into the said River Shannon between said points, between the hours of nine o'clock on Saturday morning and three o'clock on Monday morning; or between Wellesley-bridge and the Navigation Weir at Killaloe, in the county of Clare, between eight o'clock on Saturday morning and four o'clock on Monday morning.

" Prohibiting the shooting of fish in that part of River Shannon between Portumna-bridge and Shannon-bridge."

In RIVER SHANNON and CLONDERLAW BAY :—

" Regulating the use of drift nets as follows :—

" FIRST.—That no drift nets of greater length than 100 yards shall be used for the capture of salmon or trout in any part of the River Shannon between Limerick and a line drawn across the river below Askeaton, from Aughnish Point, in the county of Limerick, to Kildysart in the county of Clare.

" SECOND.—That no drift nets of greater length than 200 yards shall be used for the capture of salmon or trout in any other tidal waters of the River Shannon, or in Clonderlaw Bay.

" THIRD.—That no two or more drift nets shall be attached together in any way or be allowed to drift within 150 yards of each other in the River Shannon, or in Clonderlaw Bay.

" FOURTH.—That no drift nets below, or seaward of a line drawn across the River Shannon, from Aughnish Point, in the county of Limerick, to Kildysart, in the county of Clare, shall be used within the line of low-water mark of ordinary spring tides.

" FIFTH.—That no drift nets shall be used in Clonderlaw Bay above a line drawn from Knock to Leeknabahee, in the county of Clare.

" That no drift nets shall be used in the Rivers Maigue or Askeaton."

E 2

In Lough Ree :—

"Permitting the use of nets, having a mesh of five inches in the round, measured when the net is wet."

In River Fergus :—

"Prohibiting the fishing for salmon or trout by any means whatsoever, within a space of twenty yards from the weir wall of Ennis.

"Prohibiting the use of drift nets in the tidal parts of River."

In River Maigue :—

"Prohibiting the use of draft nets between Ferry Drawbridge and the old bridge of Adare.

"Prohibiting use of all nets, except landing nets as auxiliary to rod and line, above Railway bridge below Adare.

"Prohibiting the use of drift nets.

"Prohibiting the shooting of fish"

In Lough Derg :—

"Permitting the use of nets not exceeding twelve yards in length, with meshes of one inch from knot to knot, for the capture of fish other than salmon and trout.

"Prohibiting the use of nets (except landing nets as auxiliary to angling with rod and line) for the capture of fish other than eels, between eight o'clock in the evening and six o'clock in the morning."

In River Deel or Askeaton :—

"Prohibiting the use of drift nets.

"Prohibiting the use of all nets (except landing nets as auxiliary to angling with rod and line) for the capture of salmon or trout in that part of the river situate between Broken Bridge and the mouth of River as defined."

The principal rivers in the Limerick District, and their seasons for Netting and Angling for Salmon and Trout, are as follows :—

Rivers	Tidal Netting	Freshwater Netting, &c	Angling, Single Rod and Line.
Cashen, .	1st June to 31st August, inclusive,	Same as Tidal, .	16th March to 31st Oct., inclusive.
Clohane, .	1st April to 15th Sept., do., .	do., .	1st April to 30th Sept., do.
Deel or Askeaton, .	Not allowed, .	do , .	1st February to 30th Sept., do.
Doonbeg, .	1st May to 15th Sept., inclusive, .	do., .	1st May to 30th Sept., do.
Ennistimon or Lahinch, .	Do. do., .	do., .	Do. do.
Fergus, .	12th Feb. to 31st July, do., .	do., .	1st February to 30th Sept., do
Maigue, .	Do. do., .	do., .	20th February to 30th Sept., do.
Shannon, .	Do. do., .	do., .	1st February to 30th Sept., do.

Report.

The general state of the salmon fisheries in this district is satisfactory, though the take of fish was not so large as in previous years.

The difficulty of obtaining accurate returns of the number of fish taken is, however, considerable, from the unwillingness of the proprietors or lessees of fisheries to give returns.

During 1879 the engines used in this district were :—275 salmon rods; 51 cross lines; 28 snap nets; 77 draft nets; 112 drift nets; 21 pole nets; 37 stake nets; 1 head weir; 9 boxes or cribs; and 186 gaps or eyes for taking eels; producing a total revenue of £2,381 15s., as compared with £2,254 5s. in 1878. There was also received a sum of £85 8s. 6d. for fines.

The average weight of salmon taken was about 16 lbs., and of peale, 6 lbs. The highest price given for salmon was 2s. 6d.; the lowest 3d.

The quantity of breeding fish observed throughout the district was about the same as in 1878.

Seventy-seven water bailiffs were employed by the Conservators during the open season, and 99 during the close season.

The number of prosecutions undertaken on Constabulary information, or by the Constabulary, amounted to fifteen.

No. 9, or Galway District.

Extends from Hag's Head, in the county Clare, to Slyne Head, in the county Galway, and includes all that part of the country the waters of which flow into the coast between those two points.

Close Seasons.

The close seasons in force in the district are as follows :—

For tidal and upper waters :—

"Between 15th August and 1st February, save in Corrib or Galway river and lakes and tributaries, between 31st August and 16th February."

For angling with single rod and line :—

" Between 15th October and 1st February, save in Cashla, Doohulla, Spiddal, Ballinahinch, Crumlin, Screeb, and Inver rivers, which is between 31st October and 1st February."

Bye-laws.

The bye-laws in force are :—

In GALWAY RIVER, and LOUGHS CORRIB and MASK, and TRIBUTARIES :—

" Prohibiting the use of the instrument commonly called strokehawl or snatch, or any other such instrument.

" Prohibiting the use of nets of any kind whatsoever in any part of the rivers known as the Clare and Clare-galway or Turloughmore rivers, in the county of Galway, above the junction of said rivers with Lough Corrib.

" Prohibiting the snatching or attempting to snatch salmon in any tidal or fresh waters in the district with any kind of fish hook covered in part or in whole with any matter or thing, or uncovered."

The principal rivers in the Galway District, and their seasons for Netting and Angling for Salmon and Trout are as follows :—

Rivers		Tidal Netting.	Freshwater Netting, &c	Angling with Single Rod and Line.
Ballinahinch,	.	1st Feb. to 15th August, inclusive,	Same as Tidal, .	1st Feb. to 31st October, inclusive.
Cashla,	.	Do. do., .	do., .	Do. do.
Crumlin,	.	Do. do., .	do., .	Do. do.
Doohulla,	.	Do. do., .	do., .	Do. do.
Galway,	.	16th Feb. to 31st August, do., .	do., .	1st Feb. to 15th October, do.
Inver,	.	1st Feb. to 15th August, do., .	do., .	1st Feb. to 31st October, do.
Kilcolgan,	.	Do. do., .	do., .	1st Feb. to 15th October, do.
Spiddle,	.	Do. do., .	do., .	1st Feb. to 31st October, do.
Screeb,	.	Do. do., .	do., .	Do. do.

Report.

The general state of the salmon fisheries in this district was not satisfactory so far as the capture was concerned.

The engines used in 1879 were :—155 salmon rods ; 15 cross lines ; 12 draft nets ; 3 trammel nets ; 5 boxes or cribs ; and 20 gaps or eyes for taking eels ; producing a revenue of £295 10s., as compared with £271 in 1878.

The amount of fines received was £1 19s. 8d. ; of rates on Poor Law Valuation of several fisheries, £107 10s. ; and of subscriptions, £8.

The highest price given for salmon was 2s. 6d. ; and the lowest, 10d. per lb.

The take of salmon and grilse throughout the district has been less than in 1878.

The quantity of breeding fish observed in the district was also less than in 1878, but still there was a very good supply.

Thirty-three water bailiffs are employed by the Conservators. Of these about half are employed for three winter months only.

Upwards of 230 water bailiffs are employed by private individuals—two-thirds for three months, and the others all the year round.

Six prosecutions were instituted by the Conservators, and one by the Constabulary.

No. 10¹, or BALLINAKILL DISTRICT,

Extends from Slyne Head, co. Galway, to Pidgeon Point, co. Mayo, and includes all that part of the country the waters of which flow into the coast between those two points.

Close Seasons.

The close seasons in force are as follows :—

In tidal and fresh waters :—

" Between 31st August and 16th February, save in Louisburgh and Carrownisky rivers and estuaries, which is between 15th September and 1st July."

For angling with single rod :—

" Between 31st October and 1st February, save in Louisburgh and Carrownisky rivers, which is between 31st October and 1st July."

Bye-Laws.

(No bye-laws.)

The principal rivers in the Ballinakill District, and the seasons for Netting and Angling for Salmon or Trout are as follows :—

Rivers.	Tidal Netting	Freshwater Netting	Angling with Single Rod and Line.
Carrownisky,	1st July to 15th Sept., inclusive,	Same as Tidal,	1st July to 31st October, inclusive.
Clifden,	16th Feb. to 31st Aug., do.,	do.,	1st Feb. to 31st October, do.
Delphi,	Do. do.,	do.,	Do. do.
Dawross or Kylemore,	Do. do.,	do.,	Do. do.
Erriff,	Do. do.,	do.,	Do. do.
Louisburgh,	1st July to 15th Sept., do ,	do.,·	1st July to 31st October, do.

Report.

The general state of the salmon fisheries in this district was not satisfactory.

The engines in use, in 1879, were :—52 salmon rods, 9 draft nets, and 2 pole nets, producing a revenue of £83, as compared with £111 in 1878. To the amount produced by licence duties is to be added £2 5s. for fines, and £32 10s. subscriptions.

The average weight of salmon taken was 15 lbs. ; of peale 6 lbs.

The quantity of breeding fish observed was about the same as in 1878.

Two prosecutions were instituted by the Conservators.

Fifty water bailiffs are employed by the Conservators ; 48 of these for the close season, and 2 all the year. A few are employed by private individuals.

No. 10², or BANGOR DISTRICT,

Extends from Pidgeon Point, co. Mayo, to Benwee Head, and includes all that part of the country the waters of which flow into the coast between those two points.

Close Seasons.

The close seasons in the district are as follows :—

For tidal and fresh waters :—

"Between the 31st August and 16th February, save in Newport, Glenamoy, Burrishoole, and Owengarve Rivers and Estuaries ; for Newport River and Estuary, 31st August and 20th March ; for Glenamoy River and Estuary, 15th September and 1st May ; for Burrishoole and Owengarve and Estuaries 31st August and 16th February."

For angling with single rod and line :—

"Between 30th September and 1st May, save Burrishoole between 31st October and 1st February, Newport between 30th September and 1st May, Owengarve and Glenamoy between 31st October and 1st May, Owenmore and Munhim between 30th September and 1st February, Owenduff or Ballycroy, and Ballyveeny and Owenduff, and all rivers in Achill Island, between 31st October and 1st February."

Bye-Laws.

The bye-laws in force in this district are as follows :—

"Prohibiting the removal of gravel or sand from any part of the bed of the Owenmore River, in the County of Mayo, where the spawning of Salmon or Trout may take place.

"Permitting the use of Nets with Meshes of one and a half inches from knot to knot (to be measured along the side of the square, or six inches to be measured all round each such Mesh, such measurements being taken in the clear, when the Net is wet), within so much of the said Rivers Owenduff or Ballycroy, Owenmore and Munhim, as lies above the mouth as defined, during so much of the months of June, July, and August, as do now or at any time may form part of the Open Season for the capture of Salmon or Trout with Nets, in the said Rivers."

The following are the principal Rivers in the Bangor District, with the seasons for Netting and Angling for Salmon and Trout :—

Rivers	Tidal Netting	Fresh Netting.	Angling with Single Rod and Line.
Achill Island,	16th Feb. to 31st Aug., inclusive,	Same as Tidal,	1st Feb. to 31st October, inclusive.
Ballycroy,	Do. do.,	do.,	Do. do.
Burrishoole,	Do. do.,	do.,	Do. do.
Glenamoy,	1st May to 15th Sept , do.,	do.,	1st May to 31st October, do.
Moyour,	16th Feb. to 31st Aug., do ,	do.,.	1st May to 30th Sept., do.
Munhim,	Do. do.,	do ,	1st Feb. to 30th Sept., do.
Newport,	20th March to 31st Aug., do.,	do.,	1st May to 30th Sept., do.
Owenmore,	16th Feb. to 31st Aug , do.,	do.,	1st Feb. to 30th Sept., do.
Owengarve,	Do. do ,	do.,	1st May to 31st October, do.

Report.

The general state of the salmon fisheries in this district, so far as the capture during the year, was unsatisfactory.   The take of salmon and grilse was much less than in 1878.

The engines used, in 1879, were :—31 salmon rods, 26 draft nets, and 12 bag nets, producing a revenue of £229, as compared with £225 in 1878.   The revenue in this district has not been augmented from other sources.

The average weight of salmon taken was 9 lbs. ; of peale 5 lbs.

The highest price given for salmon was 2s. ; the lowest, 8d. per lb.

The quantity of breeding fish observed was much less than in the previous year.

No. 11, or BALLINA DISTRICT,

Extends from Benwee Head, in the county of Mayo, to Coonamore Point, in the county of Sligo, and includes all that part of the country the waters of which flow into the coast between those two points.

Close Seasons.

For tidal waters the close seasons in force are :—Netting, between 12th August and 16th March, save Palmerston and Easkey Rivers, which is between 31st August and 1st June.

For upper waters—Netting, between 31st July and 1st February, save Palmerston and Easkey Rivers, which is between 31st August and 1st June.   Angling—Between 15th September and 1st February, save Easkey river and tributaries, which is between 30th September and 1st June, and save Cloonaghmore or Palmerston River and tributaries ; the tidal parts being between 31st October and 1st February, and upper parts being between 31st October and 1st June.

Bye-Laws.

The bye-laws in force are as follows :—

" Permitting use of nets with meshes of one and a quarter inches from knot to knot to be measured along the side of the square, or five inches to be measured all round each such mesh, such measurements being taken in the clear, when the net is wet.

" Prohibiting angling for trout during April and May in each year—Loughs Conn and Cullen excepted."

Killala Bay.—" First—Prohibiting to catch or attempt to catch Salmon or Trout by means of Drift Nets inside or to the southward of a line drawn from the Boat Port at Enniscrone, in the county of Sligo, to Ross Point, in the county of Mayo.

" Second—No Drift Nets of greater length than 400 yards shall be used for the capture of Salmon or Trout in any part of the said Bay of Killala, outside or to the northward of said line.

" Third—No two or more Drift Nets shall be attached together in any way in the said Bay of Killala, or to the same boat while fishing in said Bay.

" Fourth—Whenever a Drift Net shall be used for the capture of Salmon or Trout in the said Bay of Killala, it shall be attached to a boat which shall remain over said Net while fishing, and the fishermen engaged in fishing with said Drift Net shall remain on board such boat whilst said Drift Net shall be in the water."

The principal rivers in the Ballina district and the seasons for netting and angling for salmon or trout are as follow :—

Rivers.	Tidal Netting.	Freshwater Netting.	Angling with Single Rod and Line
Ballycastle, .	16th Mar. to 12th Aug., inclusive.	1 Feb. & 31 July	1st Feb. to 15th Sept. inclusive.
Cloonaghmore or Palmerston, }	1st June to 31st Aug. do.	Same as Tidal, .	{ In tidal water, 1st Feb. to 31st Oct., and in up waters, 1st June to 31st Oct. inclusive.
Easkey, .	1st June to 31st Aug. do.	do.	1st June to 30th Sept. inclusive.
Moy, .	16th Mar. to 12th Aug. do.	1 Feb. & 31 July	1st Feb. to 15th Sept. inclusive.

Report.

The state of the salmon fisheries in the district, in 1879, does not show the improvement that the care expended on the protection of the fisheries would entitle one to expect.

The engines used in the district, in 1879, were :—73 salmon rods, 33 draft nets, 26 drift nets, 5 bag nets, 7 boxes or cribs, and 13 gaps or eyes for taking eels ; producing a revenue of £363, as compared with £451, in 1878.   There were received for fines, £40 5s. 8d. ; and £5 subscriptions.

The average weight of salmon taken was 11 lbs. ; of peale, 5¾ lbs.

The take of salmon and grilse was less than in 1878, owing to the heavy floods and dirty water, caused by the wet summer.

The quantity of breeding fish observed was considerably greater than in 1878, and the spawning season much more favourable.

One hundred and twenty-five water bailiffs are employed, during November, December, and January, for the protection of the salmon, and during April and May for the fry. A few are employed all the year round.

Two hundred and fifty water bailiffs are employed by private individuals in the same way. Almost all of these are employed by Mr. Little, Ballina.

No. 12, or SLIGO DISTRICT,

Extends from Coonamore Point, County Sligo, to Mullaghmore Point, and includes that part of the country the waters of which flow into the coast between those two points.

Close Seasons.

The close seasons in force are—for tidal waters—

"Between 19th August and 4th February, save Sligo river and Estuary, which is between 31st July and 16th January."

For fresh waters—

"Between 19th August and 4th February, save Sligo river which is between 31st July and 16th January."

For angling with single rod—

"Between 30th September and 1st February, save in Drumcliffe river and Glencar lake between 19th October and 1st February".

Bye-Laws.

The bye-laws in force are as follows :—

"Prohibiting the snatching, or attempting to snatch, salmon in Sligo river with any kind of fish-hook, covered in part or in whole, or uncovered.

"Permitting use of nets with meshes of half an inch from knot to knot, for capture of fish in Lough Doon."

The principal rivers in the Sligo district and the seasons for netting and angling for salmon or trout are as follows :—

Rivers	Tidal Netting	Freshwater Netting	Angling with Single Rod and Line.
Ballisodare, . .	4th Feb. to 19th Aug. inclusive, .	Same as Tidal, .	1st Feb. to 30th Sept. inclusive.
Drumcliffe, . .	do. . . .	do. .	1st Feb. to 19th Oct. do.
Grange, . .	do. . . .	do. .	1st Feb. to 30th Sept. do.
Sligo, . .	16th Jan. to 31st July inclusive, .	do. .	do. do.

Report.

The general state of the salmon fisheries in this district is unfavourably reported of.

The engines used, in 1879, were :—24 salmon rods ; 1 cross line ; 16 draft nets ; 1 bag net ; and 6 gaps or eyes for eels—producing a revenue of £90, as compared with £87, in 1878. In addition to the amount received for licences the sum of £8 18s. 10d. was received for fines and sale of forfeited engines.

The average weight of salmon taken was 10 lbs. ; of peale, 5 lbs.

The highest price given for salmon was 3s. ; the lowest 10d. per lb.

The take of salmon and grilse in the district was less than in 1878.

Twenty-one water bailiffs are employed by the Conservators, and forty by private individuals.

THOS. F. BRADY.

CONCLUDING OBSERVATIONS.

In former Reports we adverted to several matters which we considered well deserving the attention of the Government, particularly with reference to amendments in the Law, and to which we beg respectfully to refer.

We have the honour to be,

Your Excellency's very obedient servants,

WM. JOHNSTON.
JOS. HAYES.
THOS. F. BRADY.

ALAN HORNSBY, Secretary,

Office of Irish Fisheries, Dublin Castle,
30th June, 1880.

APPENDIX.

APPENDIX No. I.—ABSTRACT of RETURNS from COAST-GUARD of the NUMBERS of VESSELS, BOATS, and CREWS, engaged in the SEA FISHERIES in 1879.

No.	Name of District	Registering Officer	Solely engaged in Fishing — First Class (Vessels, Men, Boys)			Second Class (Vessels, Men, Boys)			Third Class (Vessels, Men, Boys)			Only partially employed in Fishing — First Class (Vessels, Men, Boys)			Second Class (Vessels, Men, Boys)			Third Class (Vessels, Men, Boys)			Totals (Vessels, Men, Boys)		
1	Dublin	Commander H. M. Darroll, R.N.																				
2	Wicklow	Commander P. B. Parker, R.N.																				
3	Wexford	Commander H. Phipps Denk, R.N.																				
4	Waterford	Commander Howard Kerr, R.N.																				
5	Youghal	Jarnal Baker, Assist Divisional Officer																				
6	Queenstown	Commander L. M. Maick, R.N.																				
7	Kinsale	Commander Edward Eade, R.N.																				
8	Skibbereen	Liett Charles Oakh, R.N.																				
9	Castletown Berehaven	William Legg, Divisional Officer																				
10	Kilrush	F. Mahony, Division'l Officer																				
11	Ballyhaigue	H. S. Fish, Divisional Officer																				
12	Scattle	Liett. Cond Harding, R.N.																				
13	Galway	Liett. John J. Hardinge, R.N.																				
14	Clifden	Liett T. H. Fabon, R.N.																				
15	Keel	Robt Geo Gibbon, Dry Officer																				
16	Belmullet	Liett T. H. Roddan, R.N.																				
17	Ballycastle, E.	Liett Alfred Anderson, R.N.																				
18	Pullendra	Charles MacDonald																				
19	Sligo	Liett F. C. R. Baker, R.N.																				
20	Killybegs	Liett C. H. H. Beckin, R.N.																				
21	Gweedore	Charles Guard, Divisional Officer																				
22	Rathmullen	Liett G. H. Dutbir, R.N.																				
23	Moville	Commander G. W. Allen, R.N.																				
24	Ballycastle, Antrim	Liett F. H. Chasman, R.N.																				
25	Carrickfergus	Commander H. W. Rochfort, R.N.																				
26	Donaghadee	Commander F. de V. Saalen, R.N.																				
27	Strangford	B. Baron, Divisional Officer																				
28	Newcastle	Thpros McGarroll, Act Div Officer																				
29	Carlingford	Liett Thos S Dickinson, R.N.																				
30	Malahide	Commander H. A. T. Simbh, R.N.																				

F

APPENDIX,
No. 2.

Abstract of
By-Laws,
Orders, &c.

APPENDIX, No. 2.

ABSTRACT of By-Laws, Orders, &c., in force on 1st January, 1880, relating to the Sea and Oyster Fisheries of Ireland.

Place affected by By-Law and Date thereof	Nature of By-Law	Place affected by By-Law and Date thereof	Nature of By-Law
	TRAWLING.	DUNGARVAN BAY, &c., &c.—continued.	May, June, July, August, and September. Also prohibiting such Nets athwart or within 200 yards of any boat, which at the time of setting such net shall be moored, and the Crew thereof engaged in Line Fishing, and to every team of such Trammel or Moored Nets shall be attached at least one floating buoy or board, upon which shall be painted in legible characters not less than one inch in length, in white upon a black ground, the Letter of the District, and the name of the Owner to which such Net belongs.
DUBLIN BAY, (10th Oct., 1842.)	Prohibiting Trawling inside lines drawn from the Bailey Light house at Howth, to the Easternmost point of the rocks called the "Maidens," thence by a straight line to the Southern point of Dalkey Island, thence by a straight line across Dalkey Sound, in the direction of the signal station on Killiney Hill.		
EAST COAST, (14th Feb., 1851.)	Prohibiting Trawling within a line drawn from the Nose of Howth, to the Eastern point of St. Patrick's Island (Skerries), thence to Clogher Head; thence to Dunany Point, thence to Cranfield Point, in the County Down.	INVER BAY, (24th Sept., 1860.)	Prohibiting the use of Trammel Nets within a to the North-east of a line drawn from the Mouth of the Bunlaghy River to Doorin Point
DUNDRUM BAY, &c. (3rd Dec., 1851.)	Prohibiting Trawling from Hellyhunter Rock, off Cranfield Point, to St. John's Point, both in the County Down.	KENMARE RIVER ESTUARY, (31st Dec., 1864.)	Permitting within the Estuary of the Kenmare River, in the County of Kerry, and eastward of a line drawn from the western point of Cod's Head, the use of Trammel and other Moored Nets for the capture of Sea Fish, from the hour of Three o'Clock in the Afternoon of any one day to the hour of Nine o'Clock in the Morning of the day next following, during the months of October, November, December, January, February, and March, in each year; and from the hour of Five o'Clock in the Afternoon of any one day to the hour of Seven o'Clock in the Morning of the day following, during the months of April, May, June, July, August, and September.
BELFAST LOUGH, (27th Nov., 1869.)	Prohibiting Trawling in that part of said Lough of Belfast comprised within a straight line drawn from the Castle of Carrickfergus, in the County of the Town of Carrickfergus, to Rockport, in the County of Down, between the hours of Six o'Clock in the Evening and Six o'Clock in the Morning, during the Months of December, January, and February.		
DONEGAL BAY, (16th Feb., 1857.)	Prohibiting Trawling within a straight line from the Bar Rock, to a place called Doorin Point		
GALWAY BAY, (9th Jan., 1854.)	When large shoals of Herrings shall have set in in the Bay, and while Boats are engaged in Drifting for Herrings or Mackerel, and when Boats shall commence Fishing for Herrings or Mackerel, that Trawl Boats shall keep a distance of three miles from them		**GENERAL.**
(31st Aug., 1877.)	Repealing By-Law, dated 22nd March, 1843, prohibiting Trawling at all times within a straight line drawn from Barna Pier to the north to Glenlough Castle on the south side of said bay.	DROGHEDA & DUNDALK DISTRICTS, (East Coast), (22nd Oct., 1873.)	Prohibiting use of Draw or Wade Nets with Meshes less than three and a half inches for capture of Fish between Bra Head and mouth of Annagassan River.
BRANDON BAY, (23rd Aug., 1860.)	Prohibiting Trawling within a line drawn from Brandon Point to Cooraha.	DUNDALK DISTRICT, STRANGFORD LOUGH, (1st Dec., 1873)	Prohibiting use of Fish-Nets for capture of Fish inside a line drawn across said Lough, from Mullog Point on the west to Ballyquintin Point on the east, between the last day of January and first day of November in each year
BANTRY BAY, (27th March, 1858.)	Prohibiting Trawling within a straight line from Crowdy Point to Carrigskye Rock; and from thence to Reenavanny Point, on the North Shore of Whiddy Island. And	SEA COAST, COUNTY DONEGAL, (30th Jan., 1874.)	Prohibiting use of Draw or Wade Nets for capture of Fish between Dunaff Head and Dunmore Head, and tidal parts of rivers flowing into the sea between said points and around the shores of Inishtrahull.
(11th Sept., 1863.)	Prohibiting Trawling between sunset and sunrise		
WATERFORD HARBOUR, (14th Dec., 1873.)	Prohibiting Trawling by Boats exceeding ten tons measurement, within a line drawn from Gaulter Cottage, County Waterford, to Broomhill Point, County Wexford	DONEGAL BAY, (21st April, 1874.)	Repealing By-law of 24th February, 1860, prohibiting use of Nets with Meshes less than one inch for capture of Fish of any kind on that part of the coast of the County Donegal inside or to the north-east and south of a line drawn from Rossan Point to Teelin Head, and from Teelin Head to Carrigan Head, and from Carrigan Head to Muckross Point, all in the Barony of Banagh and County of Donegal
WEXFORD COAST, (20th April, 1848.)	Prohibiting Trawling in all places where there are Boats engaged in Herring or Mackerel Drift Net Fishing, and that Trawl Boats shall keep at a distance of at least three miles from all boats fishing for Herrings or Mackerel, with Drift Nets. And whenever Herring or Mackerel Boats shall commence Drift Net Fishing in any place, on or off the Coast of Wexford, the Trawl Boats shall depart therefrom, and keep at least three miles distance from the Drift Net Herring or Mackerel Boats.		**OYSTERS.**
		SOUTH-EAST COAST of IRELAND from WICKLOW HEAD to CARNSORE POINT, (1st Sept., 1868.)	That the Close Time, during which it shall not be lawful to dredge for, take, catch, or destroy any Oyster or Oyster Brood, on or of the South-east coast of Ireland, between Wicklow Head and Carnsore Point, shall be between the 30th April and the 1st September in each year.
	TRAMMEL NETS.	COASTS of DUBLIN, WICKLOW, and WEXFORD, (23rd April, 1869.) Approved by Her Majesty in Council, 29th April, 1869.	Prohibiting between the 30th April and 1st September in each year the dredging for, taking, catching, or destroying any Oyster or Oyster Brood on or off any part of the East and South-East Coast of Ireland, within the distance of Twenty Miles measured from a straight line drawn from the Eastern point of Lambay Island, in the County Dublin, to Carnsore Point, in the County Wexford, outside the exclusive Fishery Limits of the British Islands
DUNGARVAN BAY, (4th July, 1848.)	Prohibiting the use of Trammel and every other Fixed or Moored Net (except Bag or other Nets for the taking of Salmon) in Dungarvan Bay, within the limit formed as follows, namely, the space lying between a line passing due East and West, through the Northernmost point of Helvick Head, and a line passing due East and West through the Southernmost point of Ballinacourty Head, in the Co. Waterford; but to the North and East of the line through Ballinacourty Head, and to the South and West of the line through Helvick Head, such Trammel or Moored Nets may be set, and remain set in the water from Three o'Clock, p.m., of one day, until Nine o'Clock, a.m., in the following day, during January, March, October, November, and December in each Year; and from Five o'Clock, p.m., of one day, to Seven o'Clock, a.m., in the following day, during	WEXFORD COAST, (8th April, 1862.)	First.—All persons engaged in fishing for or taking Oysters off the said Wexford Coast, south of Haven Point, shall cull all such Oysters as may be taken or caught; and shall not remove from any Fishing Ground or Oyster Bed any Oyster of less dimensions than three inches, at the greatest diameter thereof, and shall un-

APPENDIX, No. 2—continued.

ABSTRACT of BY-LAWS, ORDERS, &c., in force on 1st January, 1880, relating to the Sea and Oyster FISHERIES of IRELAND

Place affected by By-Law, and Date thereof.	Nature of By-Law.	Place affected by By-Law, and Date thereof.	Nature of By-Law.
WEXFORD COAST, &c.—continued	mediately thrown back into the Sea all Oysters of less dimensions than aforesaid, as well as all gravel and fragments of shells as shall be raised or taken while engaged in such fishing, and no person shall take from any Oyster Bed, Rock, Strand, or Shore, off said Wexford Coast, south of Raven Point, any Oyster of less dimensions than three inches, as the greatest diameter thereof; and any person offending in any respect against this By-Law, Rule, or Regulation shall, for each offence, forfeit and pay a sum of Two Pounds. Second—All persons are prohibited from throwing into the Sea, on any Oyster Bed, or Oyster Fishing Ground off the said Wexford Coast, the ballast of any boat, or any other matter or thing injurious or detrimental to the Oyster Fishery; and all persons acting contrary hereto shall, for each offence, forfeit and pay a sum of Two Pounds.	TRALEE BAY, &c.—continued.	or other implement for the taking of Oysters, and if, during the period aforesaid, there shall be on board any boat any such dredge or other implement for the taking of Oysters, the master or owner of such boat shall, for each such offence, forfeit and pay a sum of Two Pounds. Second—All persons engaged in fishing for or taking Oysters in said Bay of Tralee, shall call all such Oysters as may be taken or caught, and shall not remove from any Fishing Ground or Oyster Bed any Oyster of less dimensions than one inch and one-half, at the greatest diameter thereof, and shall immediately throw back into the Sea all Oysters of less dimensions than aforesaid, as well as all gravel and fragments of shells as shall be raised or taken while engaged in such fishing; and no person shall take from any rock, strand, or shore of said Bay of Tralee, by any means whatsoever, any Oyster of less dimensions than two inches and one-half, at the greatest diameter thereof; nor sell, expose for sale, give, transfer, or purchase, receive, carry, or have in his or her custody or possession, any such Oyster so taken; and any person offending in any respect against this By-Law, Rule, or Regulation shall, for such offence, forfeit and pay a sum of Two Pounds.
CORK HARBOUR, (29th Feb., 1876.)	First—That between the 1st day of May and the 1st day of September in any year, no boat shall have on board any dredge or other implement for the taking of Oysters; and if, between the periods aforesaid, there shall be on board any boat in said Cork Harbour and the Estuaries of the Rivers flowing into same, any such dredge or other implement for the taking of Oysters, the master or owner of such boat shall, for each such offence, forfeit and pay a sum of Two Pounds. Second—All persons engaged in fishing for or taking Oysters shall call all such Oysters as may be taken or caught, and shall not remove from any Fishing Ground or Oyster Bed, any Oyster of less dimensions than two inches and one-half at the greatest diameter thereof, and shall immediately throw back into the water all Oysters of less dimensions than aforesaid, as well as all gravel and fragments of shells as shall be raised or taken while engaged in such fishing, and no person shall take from any rock, strand, bed, or shore of said Cork Harbour and the Estuaries of the Rivers flowing into same, by any means whatsoever, any Oyster of less dimensions than two inches and one-half of the greatest diameter thereof; nor sell, expose for sale, give, transfer, or purchase, receive, carry, or have in his or her custody or possession any such Oyster so taken, and any person offending in any respect against this By-Law, Rule, or Regulation shall, for each offence, forfeit and pay a sum of Five Pounds. Third—All persons are prohibited from throwing into the Water, on any Oyster Bed or Oyster Fishing Ground in said Cork Harbour or the Estuaries of the Rivers flowing into same, the ballast of any boat, or any other matter or thing injurious or detrimental to the Oyster Fishery, and all persons acting contrary hereto shall, for each offence, forfeit and pay a sum of Two Pounds. Fourth—No person shall, between Sunset and Sunrise, dredge for, take, or catch any Oysters in said Cork Harbour or the Estuaries of the Rivers flowing into same; and every person acting contrary hereto shall pay a sum of Five Pounds.	RIVER SHANNON, &c. (29th Feb., 1876.)	First—That during the Close Season for Oysters, which is between the 1st May and 1st September in the said River Shannon, or in any of the Bays or Inlets thereof, no boat, in the said River Shannon, or in any of the Bays or Inlets thereof, shall have on board any dredge or other implement for the taking of Oysters, and if, during the period aforesaid, there shall be on board any boat any such dredge or other implement for the taking of Oysters, the master or owner of such boat shall, for each such offence, forfeit and pay a sum of Two Pounds. Second—All persons engaged in fishing for or taking Oysters in said River Shannon, or in any of the Bays or Inlets thereof, shall call all such Oysters as may be taken or caught, and shall not remove from any Fishing Ground or Oyster Bed any oyster of less dimensions than two inches and one-half of the greatest diameter thereof, and shall immediately throw back into the water all Oysters of less dimensions than aforesaid, as well as all gravel and fragments of shells as shall be raised or taken while engaged in such fishing; and no person shall take from any Rock, Strand, or Shore of said River Shannon, or of any of the Bays or Inlets thereof, by any means whatsoever, any Oyster of less dimensions than two inches and one-half at the greatest diameter thereof, nor sell, expose for sale, give, transfer, or purchase, receive carry, or have in his or her custody or possession any such Oysters so taken; and any person offending in any respect against this By-Law, Rule, or Regulation shall, for each offence, forfeit and pay a sum of Two Pounds. Third—All persons are hereby prohibited from throwing into the water, on any Oyster Bed or Oyster Fishing Ground in said River Shannon, or in any of the Bays or Inlets thereof, the ballast of any boat, or any other matter or thing injurious or detrimental to the Oyster Fishery; and all persons acting contrary hereto shall, for each offence, forfeit and pay a sum of Two Pounds. Fourth—No person shall, between sunset and sunrise, dredge for, take, or catch, any Oysters within said River Shannon, or within any of the Bays or Inlets thereof as aforesaid; and every person acting contrary hereto shall, for each offence, forfeit and pay a sum of Two Pounds.
KINSALE HARBOUR and BANDON RIVER, (22nd August, 1872.)	That all persons fishing for or taking Oysters in any part of the Fishing Grounds or Oyster Beds situated in Kinsale Harbour and Bandon River, in the County of Cork, shall call all such Oysters as may be taken or caught, and shall not remove from such Fishing Grounds or Oyster Beds any Oyster of less dimensions than three inches at the greatest diameter thereof, but shall immediately throw back into the water all Oysters of less dimensions than above said; and any person offending in any respect against this By-Law shall for each such offence forfeit and pay a sum of Two Pounds.	GALWAY BAY, &c. (18th August, 1877.)	That the Close Time during which it shall not be lawful to dredge for, take, catch, or destroy by any means whatsoever any Oysters or Oyster Brood on or off the Public or Natural Oyster Beds within said Galway Bay, or in any of the Bays or Inlets thereof, or off or from any of the shores or rocks thereof, shall be between the 1st day of January and the 30th day of November in each year, both said days inclusive.
TRALEE BAY, (7th Aug., 1872.)	That the Close Time during which it shall not be lawful to dredge for, take, catch, or destroy any Oysters or Oyster Brood within said Tralee Bay, or off or from any of the shores or rocks thereof shall be between the 10th day of March and the 1st day of November in each year.	(5th Nov., 1877.)	First—It shall not be lawful for any person to dredge for, take, or catch any Oysters in Galway Bay, or in any of the Bays or Inlets thereof, between the 1st day of January and
(28th Feb., 1878.)	First—That during the Close Season for Oysters in the said Bay of Tralee, no boat, in the said Bay of Tralee, shall have on board any dredge		

APPENDIX, No. 2—*continued.*

ABSTRACT of BY-LAWS, ORDERS, &c., in force on 1st January, 1880, relating to the
Sea and Oyster FISHERIES of IRELAND.

Place affected by By-Law, and Date thereof.	Nature of By-Law.	Place affected by By-Law, and Date thereof.	Nature of By-Law.
GALWAY BAY—*continued.*	the 30th day of November in each year, both days inclusive, being the Close Season for Oysters in the said Bay, Bays, and Inlets, or between Sunset and Sunrise at any Season of the year; and any person offending against this By-Law, Rule, or Regulation shall, for each such offence, forfeit and pay a sum of Three Pounds. Second—No Boat, in Galway Bay, or in any of the Bays or Inlets thereof, shall, between the 1st day of January and the 30th day of November in each year, both said days inclusive, have on board any dredge or other implement for the taking of Oysters; and the master or owner of such boat shall, for each such offence, forfeit and pay a sum of Three Pounds. Third—All persons engaged in fishing for or taking Oysters in said Galway Bay, or in any of the Bays or Inlets thereof, shall, immediately on any Oysters being brought on board any boat, cull all such Oysters as may be taken or caught, and shall immediately throw back into the water all Oysters of less dimensions than three inches at the greatest diameter thereof, as well as all gravel and fragments of shells raised or taken while engaged in such fishing, and shall not remove from any Fishing Ground or Oyster Bed any Oyster of less dimensions than three inches at the greatest diameter thereof, and no person shall take, rather, or take from any rock, strand, or shore of Galway Bay, or of any of the Bays or Inlets thereof, by any means whatsoever, any Oyster of less dimensions than three inches at the greatest diameter thereof, nor sell, expose for sale, give, transfer, or purchase, receive, carry, or have in his or her custody or possession any Oysters of less dimensions than aforesaid; and any person offending in any respect against this By-Law, Rule, or Regulation shall, for each offence, forfeit and pay a sum of Two Pounds.	SLIGO, &c., —*continued.*	Sligo, Ballysodare, and Drumcliffe Bays, by any means whatsoever, any Oyster of less dimensions than two inches and one-half, at the greatest diameter thereof, nor sell, expose for sale, give, transfer, or purchase, receive, carry, or have in his or her custody or possession any such Oysters so taken; and any person offending in any respect against this By-Law, Rule, or Regulation shall, for each offence, forfeit and pay a sum of Two Pounds. Third.—All persons are hereby prohibited from throwing into the water on any Oyster Bed, or Oyster Fishing Ground in said Sligo, Ballysodare, and Drumcliffe Bays, the ballast of any boat, or any other matter or thing injurious or detrimental to the Oyster Fishery, and all persons acting contrary hereto shall, for each offence, forfeit and pay a sum of Two Pounds. Fourth.—Every dredge or other implement for the taking of Oysters shall have a number corresponding with the number of the boat on which it is employed, or to which it belongs, stamped thereon, and all persons acting contrary hereto shall, for each offence, forfeit and pay a sum of Two Pounds.
CLEW BAY, ACHILL SOUND, BLACKSOD and BROADHAVEN Bays and the Bays connected therewith (12th April, 1877.)	Prohibiting for three years from the 1st October, 1877, the dredging for, taking, catching, or destroying, by any means whatsoever, any Oyster or Oyster Brood in any part of the said Clew Bay, Achill Sound, Blacksod and Broadhaven Bays, or in any of the Bays or Inlets thereof. And any person dredging for, taking, catching, or destroying, by any means whatsoever, any Oysters or Oyster Brood in said Bays or Inlets contrary hereto, during the period aforesaid, shall, for each offence, forfeit and pay a penalty of Five Pounds. "During the period aforesaid, no Boat shall have on board any dredge or other implement for the taking of Oysters in the said Clew Bay, Achill Sound, Blacksod and Broadhaven Bays, and the Bays or Inlets connected therewith, and if, during the period aforesaid, there shall be on board any Boat any such dredge or other implement for the taking of Oysters, the master or owner of such boat shall, for each such offence, forfeit and pay a sum of Two Pounds."	LOUGH SWILLY, &c., &c. (16th Feb., 1876.)	First.—That during the Close Season for Oysters in the said Lough Swilly, or in any of the Bays, Creeks, or Inlets thereof (which is between 1st May and 1st September), no boat, in the said Lough Swilly, or in any of the Bays, Creeks, or Inlets thereof, shall have on board any dredge or other implement for the taking of Oysters, and if, during the period aforesaid, there shall be on board any boat any such dredge or other implement for the taking of Oysters, the master or owner of such boat shall, for each such offence, forfeit and pay a sum of Two Pounds. Second.—All persons engaged in fishing for or taking Oysters in said Lough Swilly, or in any of the Bays, Creeks, or Inlets thereof, shall cull all such Oysters as may be taken or caught, and shall not remove from any Fishing Ground or Oyster Bed any Oyster of less dimensions than two inches and one-half at the greatest diameter thereof; and shall immediately throw back into the sea all Oysters of less dimensions than aforesaid, as well as all gravel and fragments of shells as shall be raised or taken while engaged in such fishing, and no person shall take from any Rock, Strand, or Shore of said Lough Swilly, or of any of the Bays, Creeks, or Inlets thereof, by any means whatsoever, any Oyster of less dimensions than two inches and one-half at the greatest diameter thereof, nor sell, expose for sale, give, transfer, or purchase, receive, carry, or have in his or her custody or possession any such Oysters of less dimensions than aforesaid, and any person offending in any respect against this By-Law, Rule, or Regulation shall, for each offence, forfeit and pay a sum of Two Pounds. Third.—All persons are hereby prohibited from throwing into the water, on any Oyster Bed, or Oyster Fishing Ground, in said Lough Swilly, or in any of the Bays, Creeks, or Inlets thereof as aforesaid, the ballast of any boat, or any other matter or thing injurious or detrimental to the Oyster Fishery, and all persons acting contrary hereto shall, for each offence, forfeit and pay a sum of Two Pounds.
SLIGO, BALLYSODARE, and DRUMCLIFFE BAYS (29th April, 1876)	First.—That during the Close Season for Oysters in the said Sligo, Ballysodare, and Drumcliffe Bays, which is between 1st May and 1st September, no boat, in the said Sligo, Ballysodare, and Drumcliffe Bays, shall have on board any dredge or other implement for the taking of Oysters, and if, during the Close Season aforesaid, there shall be on board any boat any such dredge or other implement for the taking of Oysters, the master or owner of such boat shall, for each such offence, forfeit and pay a sum of Two Pounds. Second—All persons engaged in fishing for or taking Oysters in said Sligo, Ballysodare, and Drumcliffe Bays, shall cull all such Oysters as may be taken or caught, and shall not remove from any Fishing Ground or Oyster Bed any Oyster of less dimensions than two inches and one-half, at the greatest diameter thereof, and shall immediately throw back into the water all oysters of less dimensions than aforesaid, as well as all gravel and fragments of shells as shall be raised or taken while engaged in such fishing; and no person shall take from any Rock, Strand, or Shore of said	LOUGH FOYLE, &c., &c. (25th Oct., 1878.)	First.—Between the first day of May and the first day of September in any year, that being the close time within which it is not lawful to dredge for, take, catch, or destroy any Oyster or Oyster Brood in Lough Foyle, no boat, in Lough Foyle shall have on board any dredge or other implement for the taking of Oysters; and if, between the periods aforesaid, there shall be on board any boat any such dredge or other implement for the taking of Oysters, the master or owner of such boat shall, for each such offence, forfeit and pay a sum of Two Pounds. Second.—All persons engaged in fishing for or taking Oysters in Lough Foyle shall, immediately on any Oyster being taken, cull all such Oysters as may be taken or caught, and shall immediately throw back into the sea all

ABSTRACT of BY-LAWS, ORDERS, &c., in force on 1st January, 1880, relating to the
Sea and Oyster FISHERIES of IRELAND.

Place affected by By-Law, and Date thereof.	Nature of By-Law.	Place affected by By-Law, and Date thereof.	Nature of By-Law.
LOUGH FOYLE—*continued.*	Oysters of less dimensions than three inches at the greatest diameter thereof, as well as all gravel and fragments of shells raised or taken in such fishing, and shall not remove from any Fishing Ground or Oyster Bed any Oyster of less dimensions than three inches at the greatest diameter thereof, and no person shall take from any rock, strand, or shore of Lough Foyle by any means whatsoever, any Oyster of less dimensions than three inches at the greatest diameter thereof; and no person shall sell, expose for sale, give, transfer or purchase, receive, carry, or have in his or her custody or possession, any Oyster of less dimensions than aforesaid, so taken; and any person offending in any respect against this By-Law, Rule, or Regulation shall, for each offence, forfeit and pay a sum of Two Pounds. Third.—No person shall, between sunset and sunrise, dredge for, take, or catch, any Oysters within Lough Foyle aforesaid; and every person acting contrary hereto shall, for each offence, forfeit and pay a sum of Two Pounds.	STRANGFORD LOUGH—*continued*	possession, any such Oysters so taken; and any person offending in any respect against this By-law, Rule, or Regulation shall, for each offence, forfeit and pay a sum of Two Pounds. Third.—No person shall, between sunset and sunrise, dredge for, take, or catch, any Oysters within Strangford Lough aforesaid; and every person acting contrary hereto shall, for each offence, forfeit and pay a sum of Two Pounds.
STRANGFORD LOUGH. (13th Nov., 1877.)	That the Close Time during which it shall not be lawful to dredge for, take, catch, or destroy by any means whatsoever any Oysters or Oyster Brood on or off the Public or Natural Oyster Beds within said Strangford Lough, or off or from any of the shores or rocks thereof, shall be between the 1st day of March and the 31st day of August in each year, both said days inclusive.	CARLINGFORD LOUGH. (21st June, 1877.)	Prohibiting at any time after the 1st day of November, 1877, to use for the taking of Oysters in any part of Carlingford Lough, in either of the counties of Louth and Down respectively, the instrument commonly called and known as the grope, or any other instrument or device of the like construction or nature. Any person offending against this By-Law shall forfeit and pay for each offence the sum of Four Pounds, and every such grope, or other instrument or device which shall be used contrary to this By-Law, shall be forfeited.
(31st Dec., 1877.)	First.—Between the first day of March and the first day of September in any year, that being the close time within which it is not lawful to dredge for, take, catch, or destroy any Oyster or Oyster Brood in Strangford Lough, no boat in Strangford Lough shall have on board any dredge or other implement for the taking of Oysters, and if, between the periods aforesaid, there shall be on board any boat any such dredge or other implement for the taking of Oysters, the master or owner of such boat shall, for each such offence, forfeit and pay a sum of Two Pounds. Second.—All persons engaged in fishing for or taking Oysters in Strangford Lough shall, immediately on any Oysters being brought on board any boat, cull all such Oysters as may be taken or caught; and shall not remove from any fishing ground or oyster bed any Oyster of less dimensions than two inches and one-half at the greatest diameter thereof, and shall immediately throw back into the sea all Oysters of less dimensions than aforesaid, as well as all gravel and fragments of shells raised or taken in such fishing, and no person shall take from any rock, strand or shore of Strangford Lough, by any means whatsoever, any Oyster of less dimensions than two inches and one-half at the greatest diameter thereof; and no person shall sell, expose for sale, give, transfer or purchase, receive, carry, or have in his or her custody or	(24th Nov., 1877.)	First.—Between the first day of March and the first day of November in any year, that being the close time within which it is not lawful to dredge for, take, catch, or destroy any Oyster or Oyster Brood in Carlingford Lough, no boat in Carlingford Lough shall have on board any Dredge or other implement for the taking of Oysters; and if, between the periods aforesaid, there shall be on board any boat any such Dredge or other implement for the taking of Oysters, the master or owner of each boat shall, for each such offence, forfeit and pay a sum of Two Pounds. Second.—All persons engaged in fishing for or taking Oysters in Carlingford Lough shall, immediately on any Oysters being taken cull all such Oysters as may be taken or caught, and shall immediately throw back into the sea all Oysters of less dimensions than two inches and one-half at the greatest diameter thereof, as well as all gravel and fragments of shells raised or taken in such fishing; and shall not remove from any fishing ground or oyster bed any Oyster of less dimensions than two inches and one-half at the greatest diameter thereof, and no person shall take from any rock, strand, or shore of Carlingford Lough, by any means whatsoever, any Oyster of less dimensions than two inches and one-half at the greatest diameter thereof; and no person shall sell, expose for sale, give, transfer or purchase, receive, carry or have in his or her custody or possession any Oysters of less dimensions than aforesaid so taken, and any person offending in any respect against this By-law, Rule, or Regulation shall, for each offence, forfeit and pay a sum of Two Pounds. Third.—No person shall, between sunset and sunrise, dredge for, take, or catch, any Oysters within Carlingford Lough aforesaid; and every person acting contrary hereto shall, for each offence, forfeit and pay a sum of Two Pounds.

LIST of LICENSES to Plant OYSTER BEDS *in force* on 31st December

No. of Licence	Date of Licence	Persons to whom Granted	Present Owner or Lessee	Locality of Beds	Area of Beds			Average area of beds available
					A	R	P	Acre
	County Dublin.							
73	10th July, 1867,	Richard D Kane,	Richard D Kane,	Howth Strand.	34	0	0	34
	County Wicklow.							
143	31st August, 1876,	Henry Pomeroy Truell,	Henry Pomeroy Truell,	Clonmannon Lough,	62	1	30	
	County Wexford.							
62	30th April, 1865,	William Dargan,	John Hoey,	Wexford Harbour,	70	0	0	70
150	7th January, 1875,	Thomas J. Hutchinson,	Thomas J Hutchinson,	Duncormick Estuary,	11	2	11	
	County Waterford.							
30	6th March, 1862,	Edmund Power,	Edmund Power,	Tramore Bay,	270	0	0	180
32	2nd February, 1864,	Earl Fortescue,	Earl Fortescue,	Do,	86	0	0	
41	11th November, 1864,	A. Boate,	John Kendall,	Dungarvan Harbour,	65	0	0	
134	27th October, 1874,	John Kendall,	Do,	Dungarvan Bay,	240	3	22	
	County Cork.							
4	24th February, 1849,	B. T. Brunson,	M H Morres,	Dunmanus Bay,	10	0	10	
16	30th July, 1856,	Lord Charles P P Clinton,	Lord Charles P P Clinton,	Bear Haven,	40	0	0	
24	4th October, 1859,	M C Cramer,	M C Cramer,	Oyster Haven,	20	0	0	
25	9th October, 1859,	Ebenezer Pike,	Ebenezer Pike,	Lough Mahon, Estuary of Lee	47	0	0	
38	31st October, 1864,	Robert T. Atkins,	Robert T Atkins,	Lough Hyne,	3	0	0	12
43	31st December, 1864,	Captain W F Barry,	Captain W F Barry,	Glandore Harbour,	61	0	0	61
55	1st December, 1865,	Thomas M'Carthy Collins,	Thomas M'Carthy Collins,	Roaringwater Bay,	75	0	0	77
67	10th July, 1867,	Horatio H Townsend,	Horatio H Townsend,	Skull Harbour,	200	0	0	
75	15th July, 1867,	Mrs. Elizabeth Bury,	John O'Leary,	Lough Mahon,	70	0	0	30
77	Do,	John Smyth,	John Smyth,	Midleton River,	10	3	0	
78	18th July, 1867,	Thomas Hicks,	Thomas Hicks,	Roaringwater Bay,	44	0	0	44
79	11th February, 1868,	Richard Lyons,	Richard Lyons,	Midleton Haven,	16	0	0	2
81	17th March, 1868,	Stephen Browne,	Stephen Browne,	Dunmanus Bay,	9	0	0	4
82	18th February, 1868,	Earl of Bantry,	Earl of Bantry,	Glengarriff Harbour,	50	0	0	12
95	18th June, 1868,	Mrs Catharine Bourne,	Mrs Catharine Bourne,	Courtmacsherry Bay,	80	0	0	
106	27th March, 1871,	Thomas Hicks,	Thomas Hicks,	Roaringwater Bay,	30	0	0	
117	21st June, 1872,	Earl of Bandon,	Earl of Bandon,	Dunmanus Bay,	138	3	31	
119	14th October, 1872,	H. R. Townsend,	H. R. Townsend,	Rincolisky Harbour, Roaringwater Bay.	240	3	30	900
123	6th March, 1873,	Lt Col Wm H Longfield,	S A Beamish,	Cork Harbour,	22	3	30	6
124	Do,	Thomas Hicks,	Thomas Hicks,	Roaringwater Bay,	145	0	30	
129	27th January, 1874,	Sir Henry W. Becher, bt,	Sir Henry W. Becher, bt,	Lough Hyne,	30	1	36	
145	27th December, 1876,	Standish D. O'Grady and Rev E H. Newenham	Standish D O'Grady and Rev. R. H. Newenham.	Owenboy River,	A39 / B30	1 / 3	2 / 19	27 / 16
	County Kerry.							
3	9th June, 1848,	F. H. Downing,	J Townsend Trench,	Off Dunree Point,	6	3	38	6
5	6th February, 1851,	John Mahony,	Colonel Goff,	Estuary of Kenmare River,	155	2	0	140
6	Do,	Mrs Denis Mahony,	R. J. Mahony,	Do,	147	2	0	13.50
51	17th May, 1865,	Lord Baron Ventry,	Lord Baron Ventry,	Dingle Harbour,	130	0	0	
60	20th December, 1866,	Richard Mahony,	Richard Mahony,	Kenmare Estuary,	30	0	0	1
70	15th July, 1867,	Stephen E Collis,	Stephen E Collis,	River Shannon,	919	0	0	
74	11th February, 1868,	Charles Sandes,	Charles Sandes,	River Shannon,	50	0	0	15.50
91	11th March, 1869,	Richard J Mahony,	Richard J Mahony,	Kenmare Bay,	46	0	0	7
92	Do,	Thos Kingston Sullivan,	Thos Kingston Sullivan,	Do,	105	0	0	
130	14th June, 1870,	Robert M'Cowen,	Robert M'Cowen,	Barrow Harbour,	84	1	36	10
134	29th November, 1870,	Samuel T Heard,	Samuel T Heard,	Kenmare Bay,	82	0	17	
145	Do,	Do,	Do,	Do,	117	3	15	
147	31st January, 1879,	William Creagh Hickie,	William Creagh Hickie,	River Shannon,	214	3	22	
148	6th October, 1879,	Charles Sandes,	Charles Sandes,	Do,	217	0	23	
	County Clare.							
26	16th February, 1862,	Robert W. C Reeves,	Robert W C Reeves,	Clonderlaw Bay,	119	0	0	78
44	10th June, 1864,	Colonel C. M Vandeleur,	Colonel C M Vandeleur,	Poulnasherry Bay,	190	0	0	15
56	16th July, 1867,	Robert W. C Reeves,	Robert W C Reeves,	River Shannon,	90	0	0	10
	County Galway.							
12	15th November, 1856,	J K Boswell,	William Young,	Ballyconneelly Bay,	225	0	0	25
15	21st August, 1856,	William Foreman,	John Kendall,	Ardbear Bay,	90	3	0	2
17	16th February, 1859,	Rev. A. Magee,	Rev A. Magee,	Streamstown and Clegan Bays	277	0	0	10
18	Do,	A. C. Lambert,	A C Lambert,	Killary Harbour,	114	0	0	30
19	3rd February, 1868,	Rev. B. H. Wall,	Walter S Wall,	Mannin & Ardbear Bays,	811	0	0	100

No. 3.

1879, and Substance of Reports received as to state of Beds.

No. of Licenses	Substance of Reports received as to state of Beds
	County Dublin.
73	Beds cleaned frequently Sold about six thousand, but at a loss No oysters laid down No spat remaining on beds No general remarks
	County Wicklow.
143	Nothing done since last report
	County Wexford.
68	No replies received
150	Nothing done since last report.
	County Waterford.
10	Nothing done since last report No oysters taken off except for private use None laid down No fall of spat Bed in same state No general remarks
82	Nothing done since last report A small quantity taken off for private use. Beds in same state. None laid down No general remarks
41	See No 144.
134	Efforts to cultivate oyst- unsuccessful to the present time.
	County Cork.
4	No replies received.
14	Everything removed likely to injure the spat. No oysters taken off Very little fall of spat Beds not in a satisfactory state. No general remarks.
34	No replies received
36	States that it is useless to do anything to cultivate oysters until there is some simple way of protecting them from being stolen.
45	Licenses demised
46	Nothing done since last report
46	No replies received
67	Nothing done since last report.
76	About 30,000 oysters sold No fall of spat Beds in fair condition 400,000 French oysters laid down. Many French oysters died in transit.
77	Beds cleared of mussels and dredging outside of bank About 15,000 oysters sold. Considerable fall of spat. Beds in fair condition. 20,000 French oysters laid down Few died in transit except from injury.
79	No replies received.
83	Beds well looked after. About 2,000 oysters taken off None laid down.
85	Licenses demised
83	No replies received.
90	Do
103	Do
117	Nothing done since last report Sixty-four dozen oysters taken off for private use None sold. None laid down No fall of spat Beds steadily improving as they are closely watched.
119	Nothing done since last report A few taken off Moderate fall of spat. Beds partially stocked, buoyed, and cared for Upwards of 50,000 French oysters laid down Decided improvement in size and about 30 per cent of last lot very sickly, and a considerable portion believed to have died. It is useless to let this bed
123	Nothing done since last report A small quantity of spat. Beds are in a fairly healthy state. No general remarks.
124	No replies received
129	Nothing done since last report. No oysters laid down No fall of spat Beds are in a bad state French oysters did not succeed, thinks that some vermin attack the oysters, as there are numbers of double shells empty
145	No replies received
	County Kerry.
2	Nothing done since last report Cultivation of bed abandoned for the present—the remuneration not being equivalent to the time and money devoted to it
8	Nothing done unless concrete ponds were constructed No oysters taken off None laid down Very little fall of spat Beds in same condition About 10,000 French oysters laid down None died in transit, but very few can be found on beds
6	1,500 oysters sold, none laid down No fall of spat No French oysters laid down, does not think that French oysters have succeeded, a large number having been destroyed by a small white-ish lipped whelk, which is unknown elsewhere on this coast
61	Circumstances have again induced licensee to postpone any operations in connexion with the laying down of oysters on this bed.
60	Beds kept clean Four or five hundred oysters taken off only Slight fall of spat. Bed not in flourishing condition
78	No replies received
84	Bed fairly stocked, and collectors laid down. 15,000 oysters sent to market. 300,000 Shannon oysters laid down Season cold, and unseasonable for spat Beds in favourable condition—beds picked and thoroughly carted, oysters healthy 5,000 French oysters laid down, of four different sizes, having increased considerably during the summer, considers that season was unfavourable for oyster culture.
101 / 178	Bed kept clean About 2,000 oysters sold. None laid down. Slight fall of spat. Beds not much improved
135	Has laid down 20,000 oysters from Tralee oyster bed Beds cleared of all weeds About 40,000 taken off Very little fall of spat. Considers bed very flourishing. No French oysters laid down
146	No replies received
153	Beds cleaned. 7,000 oysters laid down, making a total of 40,000 since license was issued. No fall of spat. 6,000 French oysters laid down, grown well, not fattened evenly Does not think that French oysters will prove a profitable investment.
157	This license only granted in 1879
158	This license only granted in 1879.
	County Clare.
7	No replies received
74	Beds kept clean About 10,000 oysters sold. About 40,000 laid down No fall of spat. No French oysters laid down
80	No replies received.
	County Galway
18	Nothing done since last report No oysters laid down. None taken off
16	See No 37
37	No replies received
38	3,000 more French oysters laid down. Only about 500 taken off. Slight fall of spat French oysters have only partially succeeded, owing to strength of tide.
13	No replies received

APPENDIX,
No. 3

LIST of LICENSES to Plant OYSTER BEDS *in force* on 31st December,

No. of License	Date of License	Persons to whom Granted	Present Owner or Lessee	Locality of Beds	Area of Beds	Average area of Beds available
	Co. Galway—cont.				A. R. P.	Acres
25	11th May, 1860,	Edward Browne,	Gillman Browne,	Ballanakill Harbour,	229 0 0	50
27	10th January, 1861,	William Forbes,	William Forbes,	Meenwish Bay,	226 0 0	
52	6th April, 1864,	Lord Wallscourt,	Lord Wallscourt,	Galway Bay,	1,770 0 0	100
42	1st October, 1864,	John Kendall,	John Kendall,	Ardbear & Mannin Bays,	246 0 0	14
44	31st December, 1864,	G P Archer,	Thomas Russell,	Ballinakill Harbour,	43 0 0	
46	Do,	P Macauley,	Mitchell Henry, M P	Ballinakill and Barnaderg Bays	130 0 0	140
81	24th July, 1867,	Francis J Graham,	Francis J Graham,	Barnaderg Bay,	90 0 0	1
90	4th March, 1869,	John F Nolan,	John F Nolan,	Ard Bay,	200 0 0	210
114	24th December, 1871,	Colin Hugh Thomson,	Colin Hugh Thomson,	Killery Bay,	201 2 0	40
115	8th February, 1872,	W and J St George,	W and J St George,	Galway Bay,	810 0 0	20
159	61st December, 1872,	Gillman Browne,	Gillman Browne,	Ballynakill Bay,	73 2 5	20
180	10th April, 1874,	Rev R Gibbings, D D	Rev R Gibbings, D D	Kingstown Bay,	121 2 34	
140	9th December, 1876,	Edmund O'Flaherty,	Edmund O'Flaherty,	Oranes Bay,	167 1 20	
149	20th June, 1877,	Lord Wallscourt,	Lord Wallscourt,	Galway Bay,	153 5 1	
153	26th October, 1877,	Mitchell Henry,	Mitchell Henry,	Ballynakill Harbour,	90 3 0	
	County Mayo:					
5	5th November, 1866,	W H Carter,	W H Carter,	Trawmore Bay,	19 1 11	
6	17th November, 1862,	John C Garvey,	Captain Geo Austin,	Clew Bay,	103 3 21	54
11	12th November, 1864,	Hon David Plunket,	James M'Donnell,	Killary Harbour,	245 0 0	
12	18th July, 1855,	John Richards,	John Richards,	Blacksod Bay,	60 0 0	5
21	3rd February, 1860,	Captain W Houston,	William Barber,	Killary Harbour,	43 0 0	21
22	13th February, 1860,	William M'Cormick,	W Dickson,	Achill Sound,	143 0 0	100
33	29th May, 1863,	George Clive,	Henry W Birch,	Do,	460 0 0	2
83	10th June, 1864,	A W Wyndham,	Victor C Kennedy,	Newport Bay,	20 0 0	16
34	20th September, 1864,	Captain George Austin,	Captain George Austin,	Westport Bay,	184 0 0	57
47	31st December, 1864,	Colonel F A K Gore,	Sir Chas A Gore, bart,	Killala Bay,	375 0 0	30
53	2nd November, 1865,	Marquess of Sligo,	Marquess of Sligo,	Clew Bay,	25 0 0	35
64	1st December, 1865,	Most Rev, Dr M'Hale,	Rev Thomas M'Hale, Rev Canon Bourke, Rev James M'Gee, trustees	Shores of Achill Island,	123 0 0	43
84	21st April, 1866,	Miss Anne Fowler,	Henry James F Moran,	Blacksod Bay,	21 0 0	7
90	10th July, 1867,	Mrs Elizabeth Atkinson,	J Gallagher,	Broadhaven Bay,	100 0 0	15—20
71	19th July, 1867,	Townsend Kirkwood,	Townsend Kirkwood,	Saleen Harbour,	17 0 0	16
116	29th May, 1872,	William Pike,	William Pike,	Achill Sound,	301 2 30	50
118	3rd July, 1872,	James Rowan,	James Rowan,	Do,	42 0 0	3
136	1st December, 1872,	Benjamin Whitney,	James M'Donnell,	Blacksod Bay,	31 1 17	
128	5th July, 1874,	Thomas Shaun Carter,	H T Shaun Carter,	Trawmore Bay,	629 3 22	300
129	10th August, 1874,	John Kendall,	John Kendall,	Clew Bay,	44 0 27	20
137	9th December, 1875,	Denis Bingham,	Denis Bingham,	Blacksod Bay,	60 1 4	46
140	14th January, 1876,	Michael Moran,	Michael Moran,	Clew Bay,	3 2 5	3
144	14th September, 1876,	Maria Russell,	Maria Russell,	Do,	4 1 10	1
147	27th December, 1876,	Francis Bourke,	Francis Bourke,	Elly Harbour,	93 2 0	
150	29th December, 1876,	Martin J Fagan,	Martin J Fagan,	Clew Bay,	18 2 2	10
161	Do,	Francis Mulholland,	Francis Mulholland,	Do,	13 1,20	8
151	29th October, 1878,	William Pike,	William Pike,	Achill Sound,	1,476 0 0	
152	29th October, 1878,	Daniel Conway,	Daniel Conway,	Bellacragher Bay,	2 0 34	
	County Sligo.					
7	17th November, 1862,	Thomas White,	Percy N Ross,	Ballisodare Bay,	122 1 36	10
49	13th April, 1864,	Sir Robert Gore Booth, bt,	Sir Henry W Gore Booth, bt	Drumcliff Bay,	148 3 0	40
59	1st December, 1866,	Richard J Verschoyle,	Richard J Verschoyle,	Ballisodare Bay,	54 0 0	90
60	14th June, 1867,	Sir Robert Gore Booth, bt,	Owen Blee,	Drumcliff Bay,	97 0 0	12
98	19th March, 1868,	Colonel Edward Cooper,	Colonel Edward Cooper,	Ballisodare Bay,	150 0 0	10
94	14th June, 1868,	John W Brassford,	John W Brassford,	Killala Bay,	81 0 0	
96	10th September, 1863,	Henry W Meredith,	Henry W Meredith,	Sligo Bay,	20 0 0	3
99	Do,	Owen Wynne,	Owen Wynne,	Do,	77 0 0	3
100	Do,	Do,	Do,	Do,	52 0 0	50
101	13th March, 1870,	R J Verschoyle,	R J Verschoyle,	Ballisodare Bay,	18 2 0	2
102	22nd April, 1871,	Agnes M Nicholson,	W E Barrett,	Sligo Bay,	97 3 10	35
106	24th April, 1871,	Ed Park,	Ed Park,	Milk Haven,	22 0 0	2
107	Do,	Martin Cunnawn,	Martin Cunnawn,	Do,	2 3 30	2
108	Do,	Michael Cunnawn,	Michael Cunnawn,	Do,	2 1 10	1
121	24th February, 1872,	R J Verschoyle,	R J Verschoyle,	Ballisodare Bay,	114 0 20	5
123	3rd March, 1872,	Isabella Letitia Eccles,	Isabella Letitia Eccles,	Milk Haven,	29 1 3	3
135	27th January, 1876,	Sir Geo Jones Martin,	Thomas Gardiner,	Sligo Estuary,	77 1 32	35

APPENDIX.
No. 3.

No. 3—continued.

1879, and Substance of Reports received as to state of Beds—continued.

No. of License	Substance of Reports received as to state of Beds.

County Galway—continued.

33	Beds cleaned No oysters sold, none laid down No fall of spat Beds in good condition. Few French oysters died in transit.
37	Licenses deceased No steps taken to cultivate bed.
39	No replies received.
37	Beds cleaned. No fall of spat Stock of oysters reserved.
44	No replies received
44	Bed regularly cleaned, and attended by trained staff of men Slight fall of spat Beds clean and in good condition Fishery has been properly attended for several years As yet the results are not encouraging.
11	A large number of French oysters laid down None sold French oysters failed, and injured bed.
96	Nothing done since last report. No oysters sold About 4,000 laid down Slight fall of spat Beds in fair condition. Cannot state number of French oysters laid down. Not many died in transit.
114	Beds cleaned since last report. 5,000 oysters sold. None laid down, Slight fall of spat. Beds in good condition.
115	No replies received
178	Beds cleaned 700 oysters sold None laid down No fall of spat Beds clean Many oysters died in transit
130	Nothing done since last report, beyond preservation of the bed. Slight fall of spat owing to strength of current. Delay in obtaining a lease of shore from trustees of an orphanage has prevented proper cultivation of bed.
146	Bed well cared No oysters taken off. No fall of spat No improvement in beds 9,000 French oysters laid down. One-third died in transit
147	No replies received
153	Same replies as to License No. 46.

County Mayo.

1	Merged into License No. 136, dated 5th July, 1879
9	Nothing done since last report. About 40 bushels sold No oysters laid down Little or no fall of spat Beds in fair order.
11	No replies received
19	Little or nothing done to beds since last report No oysters sold. None laid down. Small fall of spat Does not think position of bed favourable
21	Cleaning beds About 500 oysters taken off None sold. None laid down Fall of spat cannot be ascertained Tenure of license would not encourage outlay
22	Some wire and shell collectors put down. No oysters sold None laid down Condition of beds fair
71	Nothing done since last report No oysters taken off bed No spat observed owing to strength of current Area comprised within bed, being chiefly mud, oysters could not live in it, and what is fit for them is too small to go to any great expense in cultivating.
33	Nothing done since last report No oysters sold None laid down. Has made no examination as to fall of spat
30	Same reply as No 5
47	Bed has been cleaned since last report A limited supply of oysters taken off for private use None laid down Fall of spat below the average Beds in healthy condition
53	No replies received.
54	Do
64	Nothing done since last report, beyond protection of bed No oysters taken off. None laid down Considerable fall of spat. Only four or five acres out of the eleven granted, are fit for oyster propagation, even that portion is often injured by the lodgment of drift seaweed after storms
65	Beds cleaned No oysters taken off or sold None laid down Very little fall of spat. Beds in fair condition
71	Bed carefully preserved No oysters taken off About four barrels put down Fall of spat abundant Beds in excellent condition No expense spared in keeping this bed diligently looked after, and the overplus of one place strewn broadcast over the thinner places.
110	See No 161
115	Oysters carried from time to time Fall of spat inconsiderable Beds not in good state owing to drifting of sand
126	No replies received.
135	Bed carefully preserved No oysters taken off Five barrels laid down Fair fall of spat Bed in very fair order.
138	Beds kept clean No fall of spat A considerable number of oysters laid down
137	No oysters sold None laid down
140	Bed cleaned. No oysters sold Very little fall of spat Beds in good condition No general remarks
144	Bed cleared of weed No oysters taken off No oysters sold 500 laid down No fall of spat Beds in good state No French oysters laid down.
147	Beds looked after No oysters sold or taken off None laid down. A large fall of spat Beds very progressive No French oysters laid down
159	Lace moss destroyed
161	General improvements carried out. No oysters sold None put down Slight fall of spat
151	Oysters have been distributed. No oysters taken off, as beds in Achill Sound have been closed for three years. Fall of spat inconsiderable. Poor quantity of breeding oysters No French oysters laid down
172	Bed cleared of sea-weed 1,000 oysters sold None put down Almost no fall of spat. Beds in fair condition.

County Sligo.

7	Bed picked and kept cleaned. 170,000 oysters sold 751,000 French and 40,000 American oysters laid down No fall of spat Beds in good condition, but understocked 171,000, 50,000, and 90,000 French oysters laid down at different dates during past year. French oysters demasted in transit have done very well here. Last summer probably proved fatal to 40 per cent of them
49	About 47,000 French oysters have been laid down 50,000 sold. No fall of spat. The season has been very bad for spat, and the running sand, which injures the bed materially, is principally caused by the dragging of ships adjacent to the bed for bait, and by trawling
50	Bed has been cleaned, rocks removed Over 50,000 oysters have been sold Bed in prosperous condition, clean and in good order, but there is room for more stock. About 50,000 French oysters have been put down in 1877, but have gradually died off Last summer has been too cold for spat to attach.
64	No replies received
95	Shells put down to spat on No oysters sold Three barrels of American oysters laid down Beds cleaned and cultivated. No French oysters laid down. Heavy fall of spat on the American oysters.
74	No replies received.
92	Do
99	Considered it best not to do anything in 1879 except to protect bed
100	Same reply as No 96
101	Same reply as No 95
102	Old shells have been put out since last report. About 15,000 oysters sold. Hardly any fall of spat. French oysters laid down in 1876 have done very well.
106	Beds kept clean About 1,000 oysters sold. Very little fall of spat. Beds in fair condition. About 5,000 French oysters laid down
167	No replies received
168	No replies received.
171	Same replies as No 99
172	Small oysters collected. About five or six hundred used No fall of spat. No oysters put down
118	No replies received.

List of LICENSES to Plant OYSTER BEDS *in force* on 31st December,

No of License	Date of License	Persons to whom Granted	Present Owner of Lessee.	Locality of Beds.	Area of Beds.			Average size of Beds attainable.
					A.	R.	P.	Acres
	County Donegal.							
9	22nd September, 1863,	J. O. Woodhouse,	C. O. Woodhouse,	Mulroy Bay,	72	0	26	33
109	15th July, 1871,	Sir James Stewart, bart.	Owen Roe,	Do.,	104	2	21	149
110	27th July, 1871,	B Mansfield,	B. Mansfield,	Do.,	38	1	0	
								18
133	16th October, 1874,	Do.,	Do.,	Do.,	19	3	0	
143	31st March, 1877,	Alex J. R. Stewart,	Alex. J. R. Stewart,	Sheephaven,	143	2	12	
116	30th November, 1875,	Jane Moore Doherty,	Jane Moore Doherty,	Lough Foyle,	91	2	25	7
	Co. Londonderry.							
142	6th July, 1876,	The Lessees The Hon. The Irish Society	The Lessees The Hon. The Irish Society.	Lough Foyle,	3,579	3	34	360
	County Down.							
113	9th October, 1871,	Marquess of Downshire,	Marquess of Downshire,	Dundrum Bay,	30	0	2	15
131	14th September, 1874,	Samuel Maitland,	Samuel Maitland,	Strangford Lough,	15	3	30	14
	County Louth,							
10	1st July, 1854,	Burton Binden,	Lord Clermont,	Carlingford Lough,	51	2	10	
97	1st December, 1865,	John Obins Woodhouse,	C O Woodhouse,	Do,	34	0	0	
85	4th June, 1866,	Do,	Do,	Do,	36	0	0	56
97	10th September, 1868,	Lord Clermont,	Lord Clermont,	Do,	54	0	0	
111	1st July, 1871,	Arthur Hamill, q.c.,	Arthur Hamill, q.c.,	Do,	144	0	0	
				Total,	30,442	3	13	

List of OYSTER LICENCES REVOKED

Date of License.	Persons to whom granted.	Locality of Beds.	No of Acres.	Date of Revocation
County Cork.				
1857. 27th August,	Thomas Eccles,	Glengarriffe Harbour,	9	21st October, 1876.
1867. 10th July,	M. J. C. Longfield,	Roaringwater Bay,	810	7th March, 1877.
1869. 13th February,	Earl of Bantry,	Adrigole Harbour,	18	9th March, 1878.
1869. 15th March,	John Warren Payne,	Bantry Bay,	51	19th October, 1876.
1871. 22nd March,	Earl of Bantry and T. J. Leahy,	Berehaven,	123	15th March, 1878.
County Kerry.				
1860. 3rd February,	Knight of Kerry,	Valencia Harbour,	76	8th March, 1878.
1867. 10th July,	Thomas Sandes,	River Shannon,	780	26th October, 1876.
1869. 13th February,	Henry Herbert,	Kenmare Bay,	20	26th May, 1877.
1871. 27th March,	Earl of Bantry,	Ardgroom Harbour,	240	16th December, 1876.
County Galway.				
1864. 31st October,	R. E. Lynch Athy,	Galway Bay,	100	29th March, 1876.
1864. 31st October,	P. M. Lynch,	Do.	320	26th April, 1877.
1864. 31st December,	T. Young Prior,	Ballinakill Harbour,	90	16th June, 1876.
1865. 1st December,	Captain Acheson,	Do.,	18	10th April, 1876.
1865. 1st December,	Robert M'Keown,	Killary Bay,	61	10th April, 1876.
1867. 10th July,	William and James St George,	Galway Bay,	810	26th January, 1872.
1867. 10th July,	Christopher T. Redington,	Do.	600	29th March, 1876.

No. 3—*continued.*

1879, and Substance of Reports received as to state of Beds—*continued.*

No. of Letters	Substance of Reports received as to state of Beds.
	County Donegal.
9	No replies received.
107	Do
110	Quantity of vermin and other matter injurious to oysters removed. No oysters sold. None laid down. Fall of spat larger than in previous year. Large percentage of oysters killed by severe frosts, otherwise beds in satisfactory condition.
113	Same reply as No. 110.
144	No replies received.
156	3,000 French oysters put down. Very few died in transit, they seemed to be doing well.
	County Londonderry.
143	Beds carefully watched and protected, and occasional trials made to see how the oysters were doing. No fall of spat. A great many oysters perished from continued frosts.
	County Down.
117	Beds cleaned and looked after. A few oysters taken off for use occasionally. No fall of spat. Beds in fair condition. No French oysters laid down. Spat has been carried away at ebb and flow tide.
151	No replies received.
	County Louth.
10	Oysters scattered by wind and tide recollected. 4,600 sold. None put down. Has been fall of spat, but cannot state quantity. French oysters have suffered on the beds from frosts.
57	No replies received.
65	Pains made for preserving oysters during winter. About 10,000 oysters taken off. About one million and a half French oysters laid down. Some spat fell. Beds in good condition. French oysters have succeeded, and very few die in transit.
97	Same replies as No 10.
111	No replies received.

No. 4.

up to date of this Report.

Date of Licence.	Persons to whom granted.	Locality of Beds.	No of Acres.	Date of Revocation
County Mayo.				
1855. 13th April,	Marquess of Sligo,	Clew Bay,	190	28th October, 1876.
1865. 2nd November,	Law Life Assurance Society,	Do.,	118	11th January, 1877.
1865. 1st December,	Marquess of Sligo,	Do.,	25	9th October, 1876.
1866. 20th April,	Do.,	Do.,	270	9th October, 1876.
1869. 14th June,	William Little,	Killala Bay,	190	19th October, 1876.
1872. 16th December,	William O. M'Cormick,	Rathfran Bay,	95	16th January, 1877.
1873. 8th December,	Mary Fagan,	Clew Bay,	96	24th May, 1878.
County Antrim.				
1862. 3rd March,	James Walker,	Belfast Lough,	137	7th March, 1877.
County Donegal.				
1868. 31st January,	William Hart,	Lough Swilly,	790	16th February, 1890.
County Waterford.				
1864. 11th November,	John R. Dower,	Dungarvan Harbour,	27	22nd March, 1877.

APPENDIX, No 5.

HERRING FISHERY, 1879

	Boats employed, and highest number on any one day				Total Capture	Average Price.			Value
	English.	Scotch	Irish	Manx		£	s.	d.	£
Howth, between 5th June and 29th Nov., 1879,	60	187	115	37	20,534	1	5	7	26,262
Arklow, between 7th June and 20th Dec., 1879,	-	-	122	-	5,153	0	18	9	4,897
Kinsale, between 10th April and 20th Dec., 1879,	35	20	210	255	9,690	1	3	6	11,422
Greemore, between 3rd June and 25th Nov., 1879,	-	25	196	93	31,099	1	5	2	39,144
Ardglass, between 1st June and 22nd Nov., 1879,	19	218	94	19	48,745	1	0	6	49,912
Omeath and Warrenpoint, between 12th June and 6th Nov., 1879, . . .	-	-	11	35	905	1	0	8	813
Kilkeel, between 1st June and 25th Nov., 1879, .	100	70	200	30	3,190	1	5	0	3,900
Annalong, between 7th June and 15th Nov., 1879,	-	-	32	-	4,000	0	15	0	3,000
Courtown, ...	-	-	16	-	1,500	0	16	0	1,200
					123,977	1	1	0	139,880

APPENDIX No 6.

KINSALE MACKEREL FISHERY, 1879.

	Boats employed during the season	Highest number seining on any one day	Total Capture.	Average Price	Amount realised.
			Boxes.	£ s. d.	£
Irish, .	208	169			
Scotch, .	20	20	187,889	0 11 11½	100,452
Manx, .	263	246			
English, .	35	25			

APPENDIX, No. 7.

RETURN OF FISH, other than MACKEREL or HERRING, captured at KINSALE.

No. of Score.	Description	Amount realised.
		£ s. d.
385	Whiting, . .	40 1 6
758	Cod, . . .	709 1 3
936	Ling, . . .	906 2 6
19	Haddock, . .	29 14 0
11,365	Hake, ...	5,394 12 0
318	Conger, ...	219 4 0
No. of Fish 40	Turbot, . . .	14 17 6
No. of Tons 832½	Sprat, . .	787 15 0
	Total, .	8,103 7 9

APPENDIX No 8.

SUMMARY of the quantity of HERRINGS, MACKEREL, and COD. exported to undermentioned places in England, consigned from Irish Fisheries, from 1st January to 31st December, 1879.

	Herrings. No of Boxes of 1 cwt. each	Mackerel No of Boxes of 2 cwt each	Cod. No of Boxes of 2 cwt each.		Herrings. No of Boxes of 1 cwt. each.	Mackerel. No of Boxes of 2 cwt each	Cod. No of Boxes of 2 cwt each.
London,	32,969	27,004	11,300	Liverpool,	22,755	13,976	10,767
Nottingham,	3,667	2,974	4,821	Birmingham,	12,600	5,005	4,891
Bradford,	17,541	3,040	2,974				
Manchester,	9,113	11,579	11,022	Total, 1879,	120,672	78,841	55,517
Sheffield,	7,821	6,101	1,276	„ 1878,	120,906	80,299	55,546
Wolverhampton,	6,910	7,111	3,777				
Leeds,	7,276	3,063	3,499	Decrease,	234	458	29

			£ s. d.
Computing the Herrings at £1 12s. per box, the price realised in Liverpool,			192,075 4 0
„ the Mackerel, 167,689 boxes, at £1 11s. 10d. per box,* do.,			267,293 6 6
„ the Cod at £3 per box,			166,551 0 0
Total value,			£626,849 10 6

APPENDIX, No. 9.

TABLE showing Loans applied for and advanced under the Irish Reproductive Loan Fund Act during the Year 1879.

County.	Amount available in 1879.	No of Applications	No of Applicants	Amount of Loans applied for in 1879	No of Loans recommended	No of Persons to whom Loans recommended	Amount of Loans recommended in 1879	No of Loans actually issued in	Amount of Loans actually issued in 1879	Loans cancelled or not perfected No.	Loans cancelled or not perfected Amount	Instalments of Loans not taken up No	Instalments of Loans not taken up Amount.	Loans recalled for misapplication No	Loans recalled for misapplication Amount
	£ s. d.			£ s. d.			£ s. d.		£ s. d.		£ s. d.		£ s. d.		£ s. d.
Cork,	951 0 0	86	107	2,652 0 0	42	49	1,011 0 0	41	951 0 0	1	60 0 0	—	—	—	—
Kerry,	2,373 0 0	168	267	4,049 2 0	113	138	2,295 0 0	109	2,233 0 0	3	47 0 0	1	15 0 0	—	—
Leitrim,	349 0 0	3	2	40 0 0	—	—	—	—	—	—	—	—	—	—	—
Limerick,	625 0 0	—	—	—	—	—	—	—	—	—	—	—	—	—	—
Galway,	1,141 0 0	188	294	3,591 0 0	62	160	1,117 0 0	80	1,040 0 0	2	39 0 0	4	45 0 0	—	—
Sligo,	456 0 0	17	53	887 0 0	27	31	380 0 0	27	338 0 0	—	—	3	23 0 0	—	—
Mayo,	670 0 0	144	262	2,080 9 0	60	111	670 0 0	60	670 0 0	—	—	—	—	—	—
Clare,	369 0 0	33	44	523 10 0	34	30	361 0 0	23	361 0 0	1	16 0 0	1	6 0 0	—	—
Total,	6,984 0 0	668	1149	13,663 1 0	348	519	5,834 0 0	340	5,612 0 0	7	153 0 0	9	86 0 0	—	—

APPENDIX No. 10.

Table showing Total Amounts advanced on Loan, and the Total Repayments since the passing of Act to 31st December, 1879.

County.	Issued in 1874.	1875.	1876.	1877.	1878.	1879.	Total Amounts Issued to 31st December, 1879.	Total Repayments to 31st December, 1879
	£ s. d.	£ s. d.	£ s. d.	£ s. d.	£ s. d.	£ s. d.	£ s. d.	£ s. d.
Cork,	1,060 0 0	920 0 0	867 0 0	850 0 0	951 0 0	4,657 0 0	3,896 12 6	
Kerry,	2,315 0 0	1,218 0 0	114 0 0	2,304 0 0	2,233 0 0	8,184 0 0	4,793 13 6	
Leitrim,	80 0 0	80 0 0	—	—	—	80 0 0	5,119 6 0	
Limerick,	—	—	—	—	—	—	—	
Galway,	1,162 0 0	1,144 0 0	1,100 0 0	929 10 0	1,040 0 0	5,375 10 0	3,520 5 11	
Sligo,	682 0 0	124 0 0	205 0 0	267 0 0	338 0 0	1,436 0 0	812 4 9	
Mayo,	784 0 0	707 0 0	617 0 0	658 0 0	670 0 0	3,306 0 0	1,947 13 11	
Clare,	317 0 0	369 0 0	364 0 0	270 0 0	361 0 0	1,681 0 0	962 9 3	
Totals,	6,140 0 0	4,512 0 0	3,267 0 0	5,187 10 0	5,613 0 0	24,719 10 0	15,424 1 4	

*The only return received was relative to the above mentioned places, but there were 197,689 boxes captured at Kinsale, the great bulk of which was exported.

SCHEDULE of LICENCE DUTIES received by the BOARDS of CONSERVATORS for the Year 1879.

	Number and Description of Licences sold in 1877.														1879. Amount of Licence Duty.	1879. Percentage on Poor Law Valuation.	1879. Amount received for Fines, Sale of Forfeited Engines, Interest on Bank Account	1879. Amount of Subscriptions received.	1879. Total Amount received.	1879. Ave rage No. men ployed
DISTRICT.	1. Salmon Rods.	2. Cross Lines.	3. Snap Nets.	4. Draft Nets.	5. Drift Nets.	6. Trammel Nets, for Pollan.	7. Pole Nets.	8. Bag Nets.	9. Fly Nets.	10. Stake Nets.	11. Head Weirs.	12. Box, Crib, &c.	13. Gap, Eye, &c.	14. Scrapes.	15. Cochills.	16. Loop Nets.							
																	£ s. d.	£ s. d.	£ s. d.	£ s. d.	£ s. d.	
1 Dublin, .	89	2	–	18	–	–	–	–	–	–	–	–	–	–	–	–	147 0 0	—	9 16 8	—	160 16 8	201
2. Wexford, .	86	–	–	89	–	–	1	–	–	–	–	–	–	–	–	–	232 0 0	—	00 5 6	—	202 5 6	290
3. Waterford, .	226	11	341	39	68	–	–	–	4	–	4	25	–	–	–	–	1,071 10 0	—	64 12 8	—	1,136 2 8	1,773
4. Lismore, .	259	9	34	10	97	–	1	1	–	2	–	2	–	–	–	–	741 0 0	24 16 0	45 18 11	24 10 0	836 4 11	974
5. Cork, .	370	2	–	70	6	–	1	–	1	–	–	–	–	–	–	–	561 0 0	—	30 19 0	38 10 0	630 9 6	747
6. Skibbereen,	6	–	–	10	–	–	–	–	–	–	–	–	–	–	–	–	53 0 0	—	1 11 8	—	54 11 8	99
6. Bantry, .	9	–	–	10	–	–	–	–	–	–	–	–	–	–	–	–	39 0 0	—	0 19 3	—	39 19 3	60
6. Kenmare, .	20	–	–	5	–	–	1	–	–	–	–	–	1	–	–	–	65 10 0	12 6 0	0 10 0	—	69 6 0	84
7. Killarney, .	99	6	–	52	–	–	–	–	–	2	–	–	–	–	–	–	390 0 0	37 8 0	21 1 0	—	323 9 0	472
8. Limerick, .	370	51	29	77	115	–	63	–	37	1	380	–	–	–	–	2,381 15 0	2 0 0	132 10 0	—	2,516 3 9	3,052
9. Galway, .	156	12	–	18	–	3	–	–	4	–	20	–	–	–	–	–	296 10 0	107 10 0	1 19 6	8 0 0	412 19 8	800
10. Ballynakill,	62	–	–	6	–	2	–	–	–	–	–	–	–	–	–	–	83 0 0	—	2 5 0	32 10 0	117 15 0	118
10. Bangor, .	33	–	–	96	–	–	12	–	–	–	–	–	–	–	–	–	225 0 0	—	—	—	225 0 0	253
11. Ballina, .	73	–	–	38	23	–	–	6	–	–	7	18	–	–	–	–	369 0 0	—	40 6 8	5 0 0	425 5 8	440
12. Sligo, .	24	1	–	16	–	–	1	–	–	–	4	–	–	–	–	–	90 0 0	—	8 16 10	—	98 16 10	133
13. Ballyshannon,	115	6	–	48	–	1	1	–	–	4	33	–	–	–	–	–	371 10 0	—	7 5 8	5 9 16	384 5 4	683
14. Letterkenny,	43	–	–	16	6	–	–	–	1	–	1	–	–	–	–	15	164 0 0	14 0 0	12 18 8	—	190 18 8	197
15. Londonderry,	69	7	–	35	45	–	3	4	–	–	–	–	–	–	–	–	578 0 0	90 0 0	12 8 7	505 0 0	1,185 3 9	341
15. Coleraine, .	110	–	–	120	–	135	–	3	–	–	4	–	–	–	62	–	884 0 0	96 0 0	120 9 3	—	1,100 9 2	1,235
16. Ballycastle,	28	–	–	9	–	–	14	–	–	–	–	–	–	–	–	–	195 0 0	53 0 0	18 1 1	—	267 1 1	138
17. Drogheda, .	60	5	4	69	–	–	–	–	–	4	–	–	–	–	36	–	852 0 0	—	9 18 1	2 0 0	863 18 1	532
17. Dundalk, .	48	–	–	22	–	–	2	–	1	–	1	16	–	–	–	–	195 0 0	11 0 0	45 16 0	3 0 0	215 16 0	210
Total, .	2,170	113	807	761	384	138	93	46	–	96	3	2,300	2,108	10	–	–	9,890 15	442 19	640 0 6	737 19 10	11,071 14 4	11,438

The elements of the average number of men employed is made up as follows:—

Salmon Rods,	: 1 man.	Drift Nets,	: 6 men.	Fly Nets,	: 4 men.	Gap, Eye, &c.	: 3 men.
Cross Lines,	: 2 men.	Trammel Nets,	: 5 do.	Stake Nets,	: 4 do.	Sweepers,	: 6 do.
Snap Nets,	: 4 do.	Pole Nets,	: 3 do.	Head weirs,	: 1 man.	Cochills,	: 1 man.
Draft Nets,	: 5 do.	Bag Nets,	: 4 do.	Box, crib, &c. (every 5) 2 men.		Loop or Frame Nets, : 1 do

TABLE showing the Total Amount received in the various Fishery Districts from the sale of Licences between the years 1863 and 1879, inclusive.

	Amount received for Licence Duty £ s. d.		Amount received for Licence Duty £ s. d.		Amount received for Licence Duty £ s. d.
1863	5,893 7 6	1869	8,700 6 4	1875	9,417 1 8
1864	6,041 5 0	1870	7,511 15 4	1876	8,979 5 10
1865	6,792 16 6	1871	8,865 15 9	1877	9,760 15 0
1866	7,901 6 11	1872	8,998 1	1878	9,945 13 0
1867	7,317 0 0	1873	10,4	1879	9,895 14 0
1868	7,034 19 6	1874	5,418 9 8		

Increase in Licence Duty since 1863, £3,001 6s. 6d.

APPENDIX, No. 13.

Schedule of License Duties payable in each District on Engines used for Fishing for Salmon, January, 1860.

District	1. Salmon Rods.	2. Cross Lines.	3. Snap Nets	4. Draft Nets.	5. Drift Nets.	6. Trammel Nets or Pollen.	7. Pole Nets.	8. Bag Nets.	9. Fly Nets.	10. Stake Nets	11. Eel Weirs	12. Box, Crib &c.	13. Gap, Eye &c.	14. Scrapes	15. Cughilla	16. Loop Nets
1. Dublin,																
2. Wexford,																
3. Waterford,																
4. Lismore,																
5. Cork,																
6*. Skibbereen,																
6*. Bantry,																
6*. Kenmare,																
7. Killarney,																
8. Limerick,																
9. Galway,																
10*. Ballynakill,																
10*. Bangor,																
11. Ballina,																
12. Sligo,																
13. Ballyshannon,																
14. Letterkenny,																
15*. Londonderry,																
15*. Coleraine,																
16. Ballycastle,																
17*. Drogheda,																
17*. Dundalk,																

ABSTRACT of BY-LAWS, ORDERS, &c., in force on 1st January, 1880, relating to the
SALMON FISHERIES of IRELAND.

Place affected by By-Law, and Date thereof.	Nature of By-Law.	Place affected by By-Law, and Date thereof.	Nature of By-Law.
	SALMON AND TROUT. **Dublin District.**	Between Helvick Head and Ballyvotton, River Blankwater, &c. (6th Nov., 1874)	**Lismore District.** Repealing By-law of 2nd November, 1870, regulating Draft Net Fishing, and in lieu thereof providing as follows:— First.—That no Draft Nets of greater length than 200 yards shall be used for the capture of Salmon and Trout in the Rivers or Estuaries flowing into the sea between Helvick Head and Ballyvotton, or in the sea between these points. Second.—That no two or more Draft Nets when fishing shall be attached together in any way. Third.—That Draft Nets shall not be used at a less distance from each other than fifty yards in that portion of the River Blackwater situated within one mile of the mouth of the River as at present defined, each Draft Net shot and drifting to be kept at a distance of not less than fifty yards from the one preceding it on the tide and already drifting.
River Liffey. (19th Jan., 1865.)	Prohibiting the catching, or attempting to catch, Salmon with any Net of greater length than 330 yards, in that part of the River Liffey which is situated between the Weir known as the Island Bridge Weir and a line drawn due North from Poolbeg Lighthouse.		
Between Dalkey Island and Wicklow Head. (15th Oct., 1876)	Permitting use of Nets with Meshes of one inch from knot to knot for capture of Salmon or Trout between Dalkey Island and Wicklow Head.		
River Slaney. (25th March, 1854, and 4th March, 1862.)	**Wexford District.** Prohibiting, during the Close Season for Salmon, the use of Nets of any kind whatsoever, between Ferrycarrig Bridge and the Town of Enniscorthy. Prohibiting, during the Open Season for Salmon, the use of Nets with meshes of less size than one and three-quarter inches from knot to knot, between Ferrycarrig Bridge and the Town of Enniscorthy.	River Blackwater. (14th March, 1876.)	Prohibiting to use for the capture of Salmon or Trout any Draft Net in the Tidal portion of the River Blackwater, or its Tributaries, above or to the Northward of a line down a road and River from the Townland Bonaduo to the Townlands of Seaneolly and Newport Pat on the West, to the Townland and River from the West to the Townlands of Coolbegh and Ballynadash on the East, all in the County of Waterford.
Derry Water and River Derry (26th Oct., 1870)	Permitting use of Nets for the capture of Fish, having Meshes of one inch from knot to knot (to be measured along the side of the square, or four inches, to be measured all round each such Mesh, such measurements being taken in the clear when the Net is wet), in the rivers and streams following, that is to say, in the Derry Water, from its source near Killavaney to Annacurragh Bridge, with the stream flowing into same from Moyne Church through Ballinglen, and the Tomanchek River, and in the Greenisland, Shillelagh and Derry River, from the bounds of the County Carlow, flowing past Tinahely by Shillelagh to the bounds of the County Wexford, with the small streams flowing into that portion of the said river, all said rivers and streams being in the County Wicklow, for and during the months of May, June, July, and August, in each year.		
Potter River, (26th Oct., 1870)	Permitting use of Nets for the capture of Fish with Meshes of one inch from knot to knot (to be measured along the side of the square, or four inches to be measured all round each such Mesh, such measurements being taken in the clear when the Net is wet), in the tidal portion of the Potter River, situated below Brittas Bridge in the County of Wicklow.	Tidal Waters, (11th Sept., 1866.)	**Cork District.** Prohibiting the catching or attempting to catch Salmon or Trout in any Tidal Water in the Cork District with a Spear, Lyster, Otter, Strokehaul, Draw Draw, or Gaff, except when the latter instrument may be used solely to anything with Rod and Line, or for the purpose of removing Fish from any inpul Weir or Box by the Owner or Occupier thereof. Prohibiting the snatching or attempting to snatch Salmon or Trout in any Tidal or Fresh Water in the Cork District with any kind of Fish hook, covered in part or in whole with any matter or thing, or uncovered.
Owenavorragh River, (15th Feb., 1876.)	Permitting use of nets with meshes of one inch from knot to knot for capture of salmon or trout.		
Inch River, (31st Oct., 1879.)	Permitting use of Nets with Meshes of one and a quarter inches from knot to knot for capture of salmon or trout.	River Lee, Co. of the City of Cork (7th January, 1865)	Prohibiting, during the Close Season for Salmon the use of Draft Nets, or any other Net or Nets used as a Draft Net, having a foot-rope and leads or weights affixed thereon, within the following limits, viz —in that part of the River Lee, situate between Patrick's Bridge, in the City of Cork, and a line drawn across the said River Lee, from Blackrock Castle, on the south, to the Western extremity of the Townland of Dunkettle, on the North.
Bonborough Demesne, Co. Kilkenny (5th May, 1866.)	**Waterford District.** Permitting the use of Nets for the capture of Fish with Meshes of one inch from knot to knot (to be measured along the side of the square, or four inches to be measured all round each such Mesh, such measurements being taken in the clear, when the Net is wet), within the Waters in, and Rivers running through the Demesne of Bonborough, in the County of Kilkenny Provided that no Net having a less Mesh than one inch and three quarters from knot to knot, shall be used in the said Rivers during the Months of April, May, and June.	River Lee, (21st April, 1871.)	Prohibiting use of all Nets, except Landing-Nets, as auxiliary to rods and lines to part of South Channel between George IV. Bridge and Powr's Weir.
Ostrack River, (7th July, 1876.)	Permitting use of Nets with Meshes of one inch from knot to knot (to be measured along the side of the square, or four inches to be measured all round such Mesh, such measurements being taken in the clear when the Net is wet).	River Lee, (31st March, 1876)	Prohibiting the catching or attempting to catch Fish of any kind in that part of the River Lee situated between the Cork Waterworks Weir and St. Vincent's Bridge in the North Channel, and Clarke's Bridge in the South Channel, and in the mill races and in the from such channels with a Spear, Lyster, Otter, Strokehaul, Draw-draw or Gaff, except when the latter instrument may be used solely as auxiliary to angling with Rod and Line or for the purpose of removing Fish from any inpul Weir or Box by the owner or occupier thereof
River Suir, (17th Aug., 1875.)	Prohibiting use of all Engines (save single Rods and Lines) for capture of Fish between the Bridges at Suir Island and a line drawn due south across the River, and intersecting said Island at Clonmel.	River Lee & Rivers running into Cork Harbour (16th Feb., 1877.)	Prohibiting the use of Draft Nets for Salmon or Trout in any Tidal Waters made or to north of a line from Lighthouse at Roche's Point to mainland on the West.
River Suir, Nore, and Barrow, &c. (14th March, 1878.)	Prohibiting to use for the capture of Salmon or Trout any Draft Net in the tidal portions of the River Suir, Nore, and Barrow, above a line drawn across said River from Checkpoint, County Waterford on the West, in an Easterly direction to Castle Pill, in the County Wexford.	Ditto, (28th Sept., 1876.)	Prohibiting to use any Net for the capture of Salmon or Trout in any Tidal Water, made or to North of a line from Lighthouse at Roche's Point to Mainland on the West, having Meshes of greater dimensions than ten and one half inches from knot to knot, to be measured along the side of the square, or ten inches to be measured all round each such Mesh, such measurements being taken in the clear when the Net is wet
		River Lee, (28th Sept., 1877.)	Prohibiting having Nets for capture of Salmon or Trout on board any Boat, Cot, or Coracle in that part of River seaward of a line drawn due south from the Western end of Myrtle

APPENDIX, No. 14—*continued.*

ABSTRACT of BY-LAWS, ORDERS, &c., in force on 1st January, 1880, relating to the
SALMON FISHERIES of IRELAND.

Place affected by By-Law, and Date thereof	Nature of By-Law.	Place affected by Law, and Date thereof	Nature of By-Law.
River Lee—*continued*	**Cork District**—*continued.* Hills-tarrace on the north, near a place known as the Brick Fields to the opposite shore, or in the tidal part of any river flowing into River Lee, between 9 o'clock on Saturday morning and 6 o'clock on Monday morning, or in that part of said River between the line mentioned above and the point of the Custom House in the City of Cork between 9 o'clock on Saturday morning and half-past 6 o'clock on Monday morning, as in the North Channel of said River between Northgate Bridge and Wellington Bridge, or in the South Channels between the slip at Denny Bridge opposite Keyser's Hill, leading to Crosse's Green and St. Fin Barr's Quay, and the Bridge where the Western Road crosses South Channel, between 6 o'clock on Saturday morning and 6 o'clock on Monday morning.	Kenmare River—*continued.*	**Kenmare District**—*continued.* said Kenmare River or Bay of greater length than One Hundred and Thirty Yards. Second.—Prohibiting to beat the water or to throw stones or other missiles therein during the time of shooting or drafting Nets for the capture of Salmon or Trout in the said Kenmare River or Bay.
Argideen River, (12th Feb., 1869.)	Prohibiting the use of any kind whatsoever in the tidal part of the river known as the Argideen River, in the County of Cork, situated between the junction of the Owenbeg or Edward River with the said Argideen River and the Bridge of Timoleague, all in the Barony of the East Division of East Carbery, and County of Cork.	Castlemaine Estuary, (27th Oct., 1855.)	**Killarney District.** Prohibiting, during the Salmon Close Season, the use of Draft Nets having a foot-rope and leads or weights affixed thereto, in the Estuary of Castlemaine inside the Bar of Inch.
Argideen River, (15th Feb., 1877.)	Prohibiting the use of Drift Nets for Salmon or Trout in Tidal Waters inside a line from Land Point in an easterly direction to the opposite shore.	Tidal Waters, (9th Feb., 1865.)	Prohibiting the catching or attempting to catch, Salmon in any tidal water with a Spear, Lyster, Otter, Strokehaul, Draw-Draw, or Gaff, except when the latter instruments may be used solely as auxiliary to angling with rod and line, or for the purpose of removing fish from any legal Weir or Box by the owner or occupier thereof.
Bandon River, (16th Feb., 1877.)	Prohibiting the use of Drift Nets for Salmon or Trout in Tidal Waters inside a line from Stockeen Point in an easterly direction to Poulane Point.	Currane or Waterville River—Waterville Weir, (7th March, 1870.)	Permitting the space between the Bars or Basis of the lowest Boxes and of the flock or upstream side of the Boxes or Cribs of the Waterville Weir to be one and a quarter inches apart.
Bandon River, (9th Oct., 1878.)	Prohibiting for five years from the 1st January, 1879, the use of all Nets (except Landing Nets as auxiliary to angling with Rod and Line) for the capture of Salmon or Trout in any part of said River or its Tributaries, above a line drawn across the said River at right angles with the River's course from the Stream on the east side of said River, dividing the Townlands of Coolmeroon and Slacanague to the Stream on the opposite shore dividing the Townlands of Drinkeen and Knocknore.	Waterville River, (18th Feb., 1871.)	Prohibiting the use of Nets between Waterville Weir and mouth of River as defined, between twelve o'clock noon on Friday and six o'clock on Saturday morning, and between six o'clock Monday morning and twelve o'clock noon same day in each week during Open Season.
River Ilen and Baltimore Bay, (20th Sept., 1873.)	**Skibbereen District.** Prohibiting to use for the capture of Salmon or Trout any Draft Net in that part of Baltimore Bay and the Tidal waters of the River Ilen in the County of Cork, situated inside or to the North and North East of a line drawn from a point on the Townland of Clarevaun (on the mainland), to a point on the Townland of Farranreash (Sherkin Island) and inside or to the North of a line drawn from a point on the Townland of Kilmoon (Sherkin Island) to a point on the Townland of Bolymore (on the mainland).	River Shannon, Island Point, (5th Feb., 1856.)	**Limerick District.** Prohibiting Net Fishing in that part of the River Shannon between Wellesley Bridge and the Railway Bridge, between 1st June and 19th February.
River Ilen, (15th June, 1879.)	Repealing by-law dated 20th February, 1874. Permitting use of Nets with Meshes of one and a quarter inches from knot to knot for capture of Salmon or Trout.	River Shannon, (22nd Nov., 1862.)	Prohibiting Draft Nets for the capture of Fish of any kind, of a mesh less than one and three-quarter inches from knot to knot (to be measured along the side of the square, or seven inches to be measured all round each such mesh, such measurements being taken in the clear when the Net is wet) in the tidal parts of the River Shannon, or in the tidal parts of any of the Rivers flowing into the said River Shannon.
Tidal Waters, (9th March, 1870.)	**Bantry District.** Permitting use of Nets of a Mesh of one and a quarter inches from knot to knot (to be measured along the side of the square, or five inches to be measured all round each Mesh, such measurements being taken in the clear when the Net is wet), in the tidal waters of the Bantry District, which comprises the whole of the sea along the coast between Mizen Head in the County Cork and Crow Head in the same County, and around any Islands or Rocks situate off same, with the whole of the Tidways along said Coast and Rivers, and the whole of the tidal portions of the several Rivers and their Tributaries flowing into said Coast.	River Shannon, (6th May, 1865.)	Prohibiting the Fishing for Salmon or Trout by any means whatsoever, within a space of Twenty Yards from the Weir Wall of Tarmonbarry, on the River Shannon.
Glenn or Coomhola, Mealagh, or Dunmanus, Owvane, and Carrighoy Rivers, (3rd June, 1871.)	Prohibiting the use of all Nets, save Landing Nets as auxiliary to rods and lines in fresh-water portions of said Rivers.	River Shannon and Maigue, (5th June, 1867.)	Prohibiting the Shooting of Fish in that part of River Shannon between Portumna Bridge and Shannon Bridge, and also in River Maigue.
Kenmare River or Bay, (2nd Dec., 1873.)	**Kenmare District.** First.—Prohibiting to use any Net for the capture of Salmon or Trout in any part of the	River Shannon, (1st March, 1872.)	Prohibiting having Nets for capture of Salmon or Trout on board any Cot or Curragh between mouth of Shannon and Wellesley Bridge, in the city of Limerick, or in tidal parts of any rivers flowing into the said River Shannon between said hours between the hours of Nine o'clock on Saturday morning and Three o'clock on Monday morning, or between Wellesley Bridge and the Navigation Weir at Killaloe in the County of Clare, between Eight o'clock on Saturday morning and Four o'clock on Monday morning.
		Rivers Shannon, Maigue, and Askeaton and Clonderlaw Bay, (10th Nov., 1874.)	Regulating the use of Draft Nets as follows.— First.—That no Draft Nets of greater length than 100 yards shall be used for the capture of Salmon or Trout in any part of the River Shannon between Lannel and a line drawn across the River below Askeaton, from Aughinish Point, in the County of Limerick, to Kildysart, in the County of Clare. Second.—That no Drift Nets of greater length than 300 yards shall be used for the capture of Salmon or Trout in any of the tidal Waters of the River Shannon, or in Clonderlaw Bay. Third.—That no two or more Drift Nets shall be attached together in any way so as to be used to drift within 150 yards of each other in the River Shannon, or in Clonderlaw Bay. Fourth.—That no Drift Nets to be used outwards of a line drawn across the River Shannon, from Aughinish Point, in the County of Limerick, to Kildysart, in the County of Clare, shall be used within the line of low water mark of ordinary Spring Tides.

II

APPENDIX, No. 14—continued.

ABSTRACT of BY-LAWS, ORDERS, &c., in force on 1st January, 1880, relating to the SALMON FISHERIES of IRELAND.

Place affected by By-Law, and Date thereof.	Nature of By-Law.	Place affected by By-Law, and Date thereof.	Nature of By-Law.
Limerick District—continued		**Ballina District.**	
River Shannon, &c.—continued	Fifth.—That no Drift Nets shall be used in Clonderlaw Bay above a line drawn from Knock to Labasheeda, in the County of Clare. Sixth.—That no Draft Nets shall be used in the Rivers Maigue or Askeaton.	Whole District, (21st May, 1870.)	Permitting the use of Nets with Meshes of one and a quarter inches from knot to knot (to be measured along the side of the square, or five inches to be measured all round each such Mesh, such measurement being taken in the clear, when the Net is wet).
River Deel, (6th June, 1877.)	Prohibiting the use of all Nets (except Landing Nets as auxiliary to angling with rod and line) for the capture of Salmon or Trout, in that part of River situate between Broken Bridge and the mouth of River as defined.	May River and Tributaries (11th Feb., 1871.)	Prohibiting angling for Trout during April and May in each year—Loughs Conn and Cullen excepted
Lough Derg, (19th June, 1877.)	Permitting the use of Nets not exceeding 12 yards in length, with Meshes of one inch from knot to knot for the capture of fish other than Salmon or Trout.	Killala Bay, (3rd March, 1870.)	First.—Prohibiting to catch or attempt to catch Salmon or Trout by means of Drift Nets inside or to the southward of a line drawn from the Boat Port at Enniscrone in the County of Sligo to Bora Point in the County of Mayo
Ditto, (19th June, 1877.)	Prohibiting the use of Nets (except Landing Nets as auxiliary to angling with rod and line) for the capture of Fish other than Eels, between 6 o'clock in the evening and 6 o'clock in the morning.		Second.—No Drift Nets of greater length than 400 yards shall be used for the capture of Salmon or Trout in any part of the said Bay of Killala outside or to the northward of said line.
River Shannon, (22nd June, 1877.)	Repealing the first clause of By-law dated 22nd November, 1862, and in lieu thereof prohibiting between the 1st day of August, or such other day as at any time may be the first day of the Close Season in which no Fish of the Salmon or Trout kind shall be killed, destroyed, or taken by any person or by any means whatsoever (save by angling with rod and line only), and the 1st day of November in each year, the use of Draft Nets or any other Net or Nets used as a Draft Net, having a foot rope and leads or weights affixed thereto, in that part of the River Shannon situate between the Fishing Weir known as the Lax Weir and a line drawn due North and South across the said River Shannon at the Western extremity of Grannie Island.		Third.—No two or more Drift Nets shall be attached together in any way in the said Bay of Killala or to the same boat while fishing in said Bay.
			Fourth.—Whenever a Drift Net shall be used for the capture of Salmon or Trout in the said Bay of Killala it shall be attached to the boat which shall remain over said Net while fishing, and the fisherman engaged in fishing with said Drift Net shall remain on board such boat whilst said Drift Net shall be in the water.
Lough Ree, River Shannon, (27th August, 1858.)	Permitting the use of Nets in Lough Ree, having a mesh of five inches in the round, measured when the Net is wet.	**Sligo District.**	
River Fergus, (30th June, 1865.)	Prohibiting the fishing for Salmon or Trout by any means whatsoever, within a space of Twenty Yards from the Weir Wall of Ennis, on the River Fergus.	Sligo River, (1st March, 1870.)	Prohibiting the snatching or attempting to snatch Salmon in Sligo River, with any kind of Fish-hook covered in part or in whole, or uncovered.
River Fergus, (16th Dec., 1870.)	Prohibiting the use of Drift Nets in the Tidal parts of River Fergus, County Clare.	Lough Derg, (24th March, 1871.)	Permitting use of Nets with meshes of half an inch from knot to knot, for capture of Fish.
River Maigue, (17th Oct., 1864.)	Prohibiting the use of Draft Nets between Ferry Drowbridge and the old Bridge of Adare.	**Ballyshannon District.**	
Maigue River, (1st March, 1871.)	Prohibiting use of all Nets, except Landing Nets as auxiliary to rod and line, above Railway bridge below Adare.	Erne River, (15th Feb., 1871.)	Permitting use of Nets with meshes of one inch from knot to knot, for capture of River Erne.
Galway District.		Ditto, (1st June, 1872.)	Prohibiting the capture of Fish of any description with the instrument commonly called and known by the name of the Spoonbait, or any other instrument of the like nature or device during the months of January, February, and March in each year, in that part of the River Erne situated between the Falls of Belleek and a line drawn due south across the River, from the point of Castlecaldwell demesne, by the Eastern point of the Muckaugh, or White Island, to the opposite Bank, all in the County of Fermanagh.
Galway River, Lough Corrib, &c. (24th July, 1846.)	Prohibiting the use of the instrument, commonly called Snatchbait or Snatch, or any other such instrument, in River Galway, Loughs Corrib or Mask, or their Tributaries.		
Whole District, (11th Sept., 1866.)	Prohibiting the snatching or attempt to snatch Salmon in any Tidal or Fresh Water in the Galway District with any kind of Fish-hook, covered in part or in whole with any matter or thing, or uncovered.	Lower Lough Erne, (30th June, 1874.)	Permitting use of nets with meshes of one inch from knot to knot for capture of fish by persons having right to use nets in said lough, between Enniskillen and Belleek, between 1st May and first day of close season in each year.
Clare and Clare-Galway or Turlough-more Rivers, Co. Galway, (22nd Dec., 1862.)	Prohibiting the use of Nets of any kind whatsoever in any part of the Rivers known as the Clare and the Clare-Galway or Turloughmore Rivers, in the County of Galway, above the junction of the said Rivers with Lough Corrib, in the County of Galway.	Eany Water, or Inver River, (24th June, 1872.)	Permitting use of Nets for the capture of Fish with Meshes of one inch from knot to knot (to be measured along the side of the square, four inches to be measured all round each such Mesh, such measurements being taken in the clear when the Net is used), within so much of the River Eany Water, or Inver, in the County of Donegal, as lies above the mouth of said river as defined.
Bangor District.			
Owenmore River, Co. Mayo, (5th May, 1866.)	Prohibiting the removal of gravel or sand from any part of the bed of the Owenmore River, in the County of Mayo, where the spawning of Salmon or Trout may take place	**Letterkenny District.**	
Owenduff or Ballycroy, Owenmore and Mushkin Rivers, (11th Sept., 1866.)	Permitting the use of Nets with Meshes of one and a half inches from knot to knot (to be measured along the side of the square, or six inches to be measured all round such Mesh, such measurements being taken in the clear, when the Net is wet) within so much of the said Rivers Owenduff or Ballycroy, Owenmore and Mushkin, as lies above the mouth as defined during so much of the Months of June, July, and August, as do now or at any time may form part of the Open Season for the capture of Salmon or Trout, with Nets, in the said Rivers.	Owena or Bunderran River, (5th Nov., 1877.)	Permitting the use of nets for the capture of Salmon or Trout with Meshes of one inch from knot to knot in the Crana or Bunerana River, and within one mile seawards and onwards thereof.
		Londonderry District.	
		River Foyle, (28th Feb., 1871.)	Permitting the use of Nets with meshes of one inch from knot to knot in Lough Foyle and tidal parts of River.
		Baronscourt Lakes and Streams, (22nd April, 1871.)	Permitting the use of Nets for the capture of fish, other than Salmon and Trout, with meshes of half an inch from knot to knot.

ABSTRACT of BY-LAWS, ORDERS, &c., in force on 1st January, 1880, relating to the
SALMON FISHERIES of IRELAND.

Place affected by By-Law, and Date thereof.	Nature of By-Law.	Place affected by By-law, and Date thereof.	Nature of By-Law.
Tidal Waters, (5th June, 1878.)	**Londonderry District.—continued.** Prohibiting having nets for capture of Salmon or Trout in or on board any boat, cot, or curragh in the Tidal Waters of said district, which comprises the whole of the sea along the coast between Malin Head, in the County of Donegal, and the townland boundary between the lowlands of Drumagully and Downhill, in the County of Londonderry, with the whole of the tideway along said coast and rivers, and the whole of the tidal portion of the several rivers and their tributaries flowing into said coast between said points, at any time between the hours of twelve of the clock at noon on Saturday and four of the clock on Monday morning.	Tidal Waters, &c.—continued.	**Coleraine District.—continued.** Antrim, at any time between the hours of twelve of the clock at noon on Saturday and four of the clock on Monday morning. Second.—Prohibiting to have any Net for the capture of Salmon, Trout, or Pollen in or on board any boat, cot, or curragh, in Lough Neagh or Lough Beg, situated within the aforesaid District, at any time between the hours of twelve of the clock in the forenoon on Saturday and four of the clock on Monday morning.
Upper or Fresh Water portions of Rivers in District. (3rd Nov., 1879.)	Prohibiting to have in possession for the purpose of taking Fish, or with the intent to take Fish, between sunrise and sunset, at any season of the year, on or near the banks of the Upper or Fresh Water portions of any Rivers or Loughs within the said District, situated in the Counties of Londonderry, Antrim, Tyrone, Armagh, Monaghan, and Down, which comprise the fresh water portions of all Rivers and their tributaries flowing into the sea along the coast between the sea-point of the Townland Boundary between the Town lands of Downhill and Drumagully in the County of Londonderry, and the Point of Portrush in the County of Antrim, any Spear, Lyster, Strokehaul, or Gaff (except a Gaff for the purpose of being used solely as auxiliary to angling for Salmon legally with rod and line).	Upper or Fresh Water portions of Rivers in District. (3rd Dec., 1879.)	Prohibiting having in possession for the purpose of taking Fish, or with the intent to take Fish, between sunrise and sunset, at any season of the year, on or near the banks of the Upper or Fresh Water portions of any Rivers or Loughs within the said District, situated in the Counties of Tyrone, Donegal, and Londonderry, which comprise the fresh water portions of all Rivers and their tributaries flowing into the sea along the coast between Malinhead in the County of Donegal, and the Townland Boundary between the Townlands of Drumagully and Downhill in the County of Londonderry, any Spear, Lyster, Strokehaul, or Gaff (except a Gaff for the purpose of being used solely as auxiliary to angling for Salmon legally with rod and line).
Lough Neagh, (25th Feb., 1867.) Lough Neagh (27th April, 1868.)	**Coleraine District.** Prohibiting the use of Draft Nets for the capture of Pollen. Permitting Pollen to be taken by Trammel or Set Nets composed of Thread or Yarn of a fineness, not less than ten hanks to the pound weight, doubled and twisted with a mesh of net less than one inch from knot to knot, from the 1st of March to the 19th August.	Lough Neagh, (30th Dec., 1879.)	Prohibiting having any Net for the capture of Salmon, Trout, or Pollen, in or on board any boat, cot, or curragh, in Lough Neagh, in said District, during the annual Close Season for Salmon, Trout, and Pollen, in said Lough Neagh.
Whole District, (17th Oct., 1878.) Tidal Waters, and Loughs Neagh and Beg, (16th Dec., 1878.)	Prohibiting snatching or attempting to snatch Salmon in any of the tidal or fresh waters of District. First.—Prohibiting to have any Net for the capture of Salmon or Trout, in or on board any boat, cot, or curragh, in the Tidal Waters of said District, which comprises the tidal portions of all Rivers and their tributaries flowing into the sea along the coast between the sea-point of the Townland Boundary between the Townlands of Downhill and Drumagully in the County of Londonderry, and the Point of Portrush in the County of	Bush River, (28th Feb., 1870.)	**Ballycastle District.** Repealing Demolition of Bush River Estuary as fixed by the late Special Commissioners on 8th Feb., 1864.
		Between Clogher Head and Ballaghan Point (20th April, 1872.)	**Dundalk District.** Prohibiting to catch or attempting to catch Salmon or Trout with any Net of greater length than 300 Yards on that part of the Sea Coast situated between Clogher Head and Ballaghan Point, in the County of Louth.
		Tidal Waters, (30th June, 1873.)	Prohibiting the snatching or attempting to snatch Salmon in any Tidal water of District between Dunany Point and Soldier's Point, in the County Louth, with a Spear, Lyster, Otter, Strokehaul, Draw-draw, or Gaff, except when the latter may be used solely as auxiliary to angling with Rod and Line, or for removing fish from any legal Weir or Box by the Owner or Occupier thereof. ...

APPENDIX,

TABLE showing the CLOSE SEASONS for SALMON and TROUT in

No. and Name of District.	Boundary of District.	Total.
1. Dublin	Skerries to Wicklow.	From Howth to Dalkey Island, between 14th August and 1st February. For remainder of District, between 18th September and 2nd March.
2. Wexford	Wicklow to Kiln Bay, East of Bannow Bay.	Between 15th September and 20th April.
3. Waterford	Kiln Bay to Helvick Head.	" 10th August and 1st February.
4. Lismore	Helvick Head to Ballycotton.	" 31st August and 16th February.
5. Cork	Ballycotton Head to Galley Head.	15th August and the 18th of Feb., save in Bandon and Argideen Rivers, between 15th August and 1st March for Bandon, and between 31st August and 1st March for Argideen
6. Skibbereen	Galley Head to Mizen Head.	" 14th September and 1st May.
6a. Bantry	Mizen Head to Crow Head.	" 30th September and 1st May.
6b. Kenmare	Crow Head to Lamb Head.	15th September and 1st April.
7. Killarney	Lamb Head to Dunmore Head, including Blaskets.	31st July and 16th January save Rivers Maine, Ferta, or Valencia, Inny, and Waterville, and their Tributaries. Maine, Ferta or Valencia, Inny, and Tributaries, between 15th September and 1st May. Waterville and its Tributaries, between 16th July and 1st January.
8. Limerick	Dunmore to Hags Head	Between 31st July and 12th February, save River Cashen and Tributaries, and save between Kerry Head and Dunmore Head, and between Loop Head and Hags Head, and all Rivers running into the sea between these points For River Cashen down to its Mouth and Tributaries, between 31st August and 1st June Between Dunmore Head and Kerry Head, and all Rivers flowing into sea between these points, between 15th September and 1st April Between Loop Head and Hags Head, and all Rivers running into the sea between these points, between 15th September and 1st May.
9. Galway	Hags Head to Slyne Head.	Between 14th August and 1st February, save in Corrib or Galway River and Lakes and Tributaries, which is between 31st August and 10th February.
10a. Ballinakill	Slyne Head to Pigeon Point.	Between the 31st of August and 16th of February, save in Lenaburgh and Carrowkelly Rivers and Maneries For Lenaburgh and Carrowkelly Rivers and Estuaries, between 15th of September and 1st July
10b. Bangor	Pigeon Point to Benwee Head.	Between 31st August and 16th February, save in Newport and Glenamoy, Burrishoole and Owengarve Rivers and Estuaries. For Newport River and Estuary, 31st August and 20th March, Glenamoy River and Estuary, 15th September and 1st May, Burrishoole and Owengarve River and Estuaries, 31st August and 16th February.
11. Ballina	Benwee to Coonamore.	Between 12th August and 16th March, save Palmerston and Easkey Rivers, which is between 31st August and 1st June.
12. Sligo	Coonamore to Mullaghmore	" 19th August and 4th February, save Slape River, its Estuary and Tributaries, which is between 31st July and 10th January.
13. Ballyshannon	Mullaghmore to Rosan.	" 19th August and 1st March, save River Eske and Tributaries, which is between 17th September and 1st April.
14. Letterkenny	Rosan to Malin Head.	" 19th August and 4th Feb., and one mile above Fahway, rive Cruss or Bunorann, and Gweebarra Rivers. For Cruss or Bunorann River, between 14th September and 15th April, for Gweebarra, between 30th Sept and 1st April.
15a. Londonderry	Malin to Dowahill Boundary.	Between 31st August and 15th April.
15b. Coleraine	Dowahill Boundary to Portrush.	" 19th August and 4th February.
16. Ballycastle	Portrush to Donaghadee.	" Do. do
17a. Drogheda	Skerries to Clogher Head.	" 4th August and 12th February
17b. Dundalk	Clogher Head to Donaghadee.	" 31st August and 1st April, save in Annagassan, Glyde, Dee, and Fane Rivers. In Glyde, Dee, and Annagassan Rivers, between 19th August and 12th February, in Fane River between 19th August and 1st April.

NOTE.— The 21st section of the 26th & 27th Vic. c. 114, requires there shall not be fewer than 168 days Close Season in each Fishery.
WEEKLY CLOSE SEASON.—By the 24th section of the 26th & 27th Vic. c. 114, no Salmon or Trout shall be taken by net or taken in any way, except by single Rod and Line, between six of the clock on Saturday morning and six of the clock on the succeeding Monday morning.

No. 15.

the different Districts in Ireland on 31st December, 1879

No.	Fresh Water.	Angling with Cross Lines.	Angling with Single Rod and Line	Date of last change.	Principal Rivers in District.
1	Same as Tidal.	Same as Netting.	Between 31st Oct. & 1st day of Feb	13th Oct. 1874.	1. Liffey, Bray, Vartry.
2	Same as Tidal.	Same as Netting.	Between 30th Sept and 15th March	29th Dec. 1873	2. Slaney, Courtown, Inch, Urrin, Bann.
3	Same as Tidal.	Same as Netting.	Between 10th Sept and 1st Feb, save River Suir and Tributaries, between 15th Sept and 1st Feb	12th Nov. 1874. 4th Oct. 1879.	3. Suir, Nore, and Barrow
4	Same as Tidal.	Same as Netting.	Between 12th Oct and 15th Feb	16th Dec. 1875	4. Blackwater.
5	Same as Tidal.	Same as Netting.	Between 12th Oct and 15th of Feb	20th Dec. 1874.	5. Lee Bandon, Argideen
6	Between 31st July and 1st May.	Same as Netting.	Between 31st Oct. and 17th March	30th June, 1878	6. Salmon rita, Sheen, &c
9	Same as Tidal.	Same as Netting.	Do. do.	29th Jan, 1874.	6*. Iten

(table continues, heavily illegible)

APPENDIX,
No. 16

Certificates
for Fixed
Engines.

APPENDIX,

CERTIFICATES granted up to 31st December, 1879, for Fixed Engines for

No.	Place.	Name of Person in whose Certificate granted.	Date of Certificate.	District in which Net situated.	Description of Fixed Net.
65	River Moy,	Mary Anne Little and Andrew Clarke,	2 May, 1870,	Ballina,	6 Fixed draft nets
67	Ditto,	J. W. Stratford,	13 May, 1870,	Ditto,	3 Ditto,
68	Sea off coast, co. Mayo,	William Little,	5 June, 1870,	Ditto,	2 Bag nets,
108	Sea off coast, co. Sligo,	William Little,	16 May, 1872,	Ditto,	3 Ditto,
2	Sea off co. Antrim,	A. G. Fullerton,	5 September, 1865,	Ballycastle,	1 Ditto,
3	Ditto,	Ditto,	Ditto,	Ditto,	1 Ditto,
5	Ditto,	Thomas Black,	2 October, 1865,	Ditto,	1 Ditto,
6	Ditto,	Ditto,	Ditto,	Ditto,	1 Ditto,
7	Ditto,	Sir E. MacNaghten,	Ditto,	Ditto,	1 Ditto,
8	Ditto,	Thomas Black,	Ditto,	Ditto,	1 Ditto,
9	Ditto,	Earl of Antrim,	22 November, 1865,	Ditto,	1 Ditto,
10	Ditto,	Thomas Black,	2 October, 1865,	Ditto,	1 Ditto,
11	Ditto,	Ditto,	21 October, 1865,	Ditto,	1 Ditto,
14	Ditto,	J. C. Anderson,	26 October, 1865,	Ditto,	1 Ditto,
15	Ditto,	Ditto,	Ditto,	Ditto,	1 Ditto,
59	Cushlough Bay,	Earl of Antrim,	6 February, 1870,	Ditto,	1 Ditto,
58	Off coast, co. Antrim,	Sir E. W. Macnaghten, bart.	3 May, 1870,	Ditto,	1 Ditto,
60	Ditto,	Ditto,	Ditto,	Ditto,	1 Ditto,
61	Ditto,	Ditto,	Ditto,	Ditto,	Fixed draft net,
66	Ballycastle Bay,	Sir H. H. Boyd, bart,	Ditto,	Ditto,	1 Ditto,
*70	Sea off coast, co. Antrim,	Denis Black,	11 May, 1870,	Ditto,	1 Ditto,
71	Ditto,	John Fraly,	Ditto,	Ditto,	1 Ditto,
72	Ditto,	John M'Coldroney,	Ditto,	Ditto,	1 Ditto,
73	Ditto,	Edmond M'Neill,	Ditto,	Ditto,	1 Ditto,
74	Red Bay,	H. M'Neill,	Ditto,	Ditto,	1 Ditto,
75	Sea off coast, co. Antrim,	Earl of Antrim,	Ditto,	Ditto,	1 Ditto,
82	Ditto,	Lady Boyd, on behalf of Sir H. H. Boyd, bart.	Ditto,	Ditto,	1 Ditto,
84	Ditto,	J. E. Leslie,	Ditto,	Ditto,	1 Ditto,
97	Ditto,	Earl of Antrim,	29 April, 1871,	Ditto,	1 Ditto,
100	Ditto,	Denis Black,	19 July, 1871,	Ditto,	1 Ditto,
116	Ditto,	John Finlay,	9 July, 1872,	Ditto,	1 Ditto,
117	Ditto,	Robert Woodside,	10 July, 1872,	Ditto,	1 Ditto,
33	River Erne,	B. L. Moore, S. M. Moore, and S. M. Alexander	29 October, 1879,	Ballyshannon,	1 Stake net,
64	Sea off Coast of Sligo,	Hon A. L. M. Ashley,	Ditto,	Ditto,	1 Fixed draft net,
76	Sea off coast, co. Donegal,	H. G. Murray Stewart,	13 May, 1870,	Ditto,	2 Ditto,
79	Inver Bay,	William Sinclair,	Ditto,	Ditto,	2 Ditto,
80	Sea off coast, co. Donegal,	Marquis Conyngham,	Ditto,	Ditto,	1 Ditto,
93	Ditto,	Eleanora Bustard,	Ditto,	Ditto,	1 Ditto,
90	River Erne,	B. L. Moore and others,	7 February, 1871,	Ditto,	3 Ditto,
62	Island of Achill,	Alexander Hector,	2 May, 1870,	Bangor,	1 Bag net,
68	Owenmore River,	William Pateno,	18 May, 1870,	Ditto,	3 Fixed draft nets,
69	Owenmore and Ballycroy Rivers,	Helen Little,	19 May, 1870,	Ditto,	7 Ditto,
110	Sea off coast, co. Mayo,	Sir P. A. K. Gore, bart,	25 May, 1872,	Ditto,	2 Bag nets,
111	Ditto,	William Pike,	1 July, 1872,	Ditto,	2 Ditto,
112	Ditto,	Trustees Achill Mission,	Ditto,	Ditto,	1 Ditto,
113	Ditto,	Ditto,	Ditto,	Ditto,	1 Ditto,
114	Ditto,	Ditto,	Ditto,	Ditto,	3 Ditto,
128	Ditto,	C S S Dickke,	18 December, 1879,	Ditto,	3 Ditto,
1	Sea off co. Londonderry,	Henry O'Neill,	31 August, 1865,	Coleraine,	Bag Net,
12	Sea off co. Antrim,	Thomas Black,	21 October, 1865,	Ditto,	Ditto,
32	Bann River,	The Irish Society,	15 February, 1871,	Ditto,	4 Fixed draft nets
24	Kingshole Bay,	Samuel Hodder,	7 March, 1867,	Cork,	1 Bag Net,
36	Cork Harbour,	Sampson French,	23 September, 1870,	Ditto,	1 Stake net,
119	Ditto,	John Charles Bennett,	23 December, 1876,	Ditto,	1 Ditto,
13	Sea off co. Louth,	Sir Alan R. Bellingham,	28 October, 1865,	Dundalk,	1 Head Weir,
16	Ditto,	John P Jones,	16 November, 1865,	Ditto,	1 Bag Net,
115	Ditto,	Arthur Newcoman,	10 July, 1872,	Ditto,	1 Ditto,
4	Kenmare River,	B B Hartopp,	16 January, 1866,	Kenmare,	1 Ditto,
127	Kenmare Bay,	P. C. Hland,	16 January, 1880,	Ditto,	1 Ditto,
61	River Leannan (Estuary),	Sir J. Stewart, bart,	13 May, 1870,	Letterkenny,	Fixed draft net,
118	Sea off coast, co. Donegal,	Charles F Stewart,	19 June, 1874,	Ditto,	1 Bag nets,
121	Estuary of Crana or Castle River,	Alexander A Richardson,	2 October, 1877,	Ditto,	Fixed draft net,
17	River Shannon,	William B Barrington,	7 November, 1865,	Limerick,	1 Fly Net,
24	Ditto,	B Cunningham,	16 March, 1866,	Ditto,	1 Stake Net,
25	River Brawray,	Thomas Studdert,	11 February, 1867,	Ditto,	1 Head Weir,
31	Doonmore Strand,	John Scott,	18 May, 1869,	Ditto,	1 Salmon Weir or Well.
33	Doonbeg Strand,	W. Stackpole,	Ditto,	Ditto,	1 Ditto,
35	Shannon,	William Creagh Hickie,	8 February, 1870,	Ditto,	1 Stake net,
36	Ditto,	Colonel C. M. Vandeleur,	Ditto,	Ditto,	1 Ditto,
37	Clonderlaw Bay,	Lord Ansaly,	Ditto,	Ditto,	1 Ditto,
38	Ditto,	Ditto,	Ditto,	Ditto,	1 Ditto,
39	Ditto,		Ditto,	Ditto,	1 Ditto,
40	Ditto,	R. W C. Reeves,	Ditto,	Ditto,	1 Ditto,
41	Ditto,	Ditto,	Ditto,	Ditto,	1 Ditto,
42	Ditto,	Ditto,	Ditto,	Ditto,	1 Ditto,
43	Ditto,	Ditto,	Ditto,	Ditto,	1 Ditto,
44	Shannon,	Knight of Glin,	Ditto,	Ditto,	1 Ditto,
45	Ditto,	C H Minchin,	Ditto,	Ditto,	1 Ditto,
46	Clonderlaw Bay,	Col H. Haldmon,	Ditto,	Ditto,	1 Ditto,
49	Shannon,	John Griffin,	Ditto,	Ditto,	1 Ditto,
52	Ditto,	Leslie Wren,	Ditto,	Ditto,	1 Ditto,
53	Ditto,	Ditto,	Ditto,	Ditto,	1 Ditto,

* This certificate lapsed

Appendix, No. 16.

Certificates for Fixed Engines.

No. 16.

fishing for Salmon or Trout (arranged in Districts).

No.	Particulars of Size, &c.	Observations.
65	6 nets, from 150 to 250 yards in length,	—
67	3 nets, not exceeding 80 yards in length,	Sparmore fixed nets.
85	Leaders, 50 fathoms long each; and each bag about 7 feet wide,	Kilcummin bag nets.
109	Leaders, each 80 fathoms long; heads, 6 fathoms each,	Ennacrone nets.
2	Leader, 72 yards; net, 20 yards,	Larrybane net.
3	Leader, 50 yards; net, 20 yards,	Carrickarade net.
5	Leader, 600 feet, net, 66 feet,	Curran net
6	Leader, 480 feet; net, 66 feet,	Big Duncan net.
7	Leader, 246 feet, net, 84 feet,	Portbraddan net.
8	Leader, 480 feet; net, 66 feet,	Skerryvon net.
9	Leader, 150 feet, net, 48 feet,	Tan net.
10	Leader, 240 feet, net, 66 feet,	Little Duncan net.
11	Leader, 288 feet; net, 66 feet,	Portmoon net.
14	Net, 516 feet, head, 48 feet,	Portfad net.
15	Ditto, ditto,	Portmoon net.
50	Leader, 113 yards long; head 48 feet long,	Caralough net.
59	Leader, 93 yards long; head, 21 yards long,	Blackrock bag net.
60	Leader, 74 yards long; head, 21 yards long,	Glashan Island bag net.
61	Length, 180 yards,	Cregmacagh net.
65	Length, 100 yards,	Ballycastle net.
70	Length, 300 feet,	Moneyvart fixed draft net.
71	Length, 80 yards,	Ballylaaran fixed net.
72	Length, 104 yards,	Clarepark fixed net.
73	Length, 90 yards,	Curryshaskin fixed net.
74	Length, 116 yards,	Red Bay fixed draft net.
75	Length, 100 yards,	Layd fixed draft net.
63	Length, 90 yards,	Kinbane net.
64	Length, 75 yards,	Templastragh net.
97	120 yards long,	Pier net
100	Length, 100 yards,	Moneyvart, otherwise Portvinagar, draft net.
116	48 fathoms long,	Skons net.
117	Leader, 74 yards long; head, 26 yards long,	Cregganboy net.
23	Lead arm, 210 yards fixed,	Kine weir.
84	Length, 120 yards long,	Mullaghmore net
78	2 nets, not exceeding 250 yards in length,	Mocklecas & Gortalan nets
79	2 nets, 140 yards long,	Inver nets
80	Length, 180 yards,	Ballyederlane net.
83	Length, 90 yards,	Drumbanan net.
90	Each 200 yards long,	—
62	Leader, 150 yards long; head, 18 yards long,	Keel net
68	3 nets, not exceeding 120 yards in length,	Owenmore nets.
69	7 Ditto, 300 ditto,	Tullaghan nets
110	Leaders, 40 fathoms long; heads, 5 fathoms long,	Cuskleeka and Dooghbeg nets
111	Leaders, 40 fathoms long, and heads 5 fathoms long,	Dooega nets
112	Leaders, 40 fathoms, heads, 5 fathoms long,	Slievemore nets.
113	Leaders, 40 fathoms long, head, 5 fathoms long,	Doogort nets.
114	Ditto, ditto,	Keel nets
126	Leaders of each not exceeding 40 fathoms long, heads, 3 fathoms long; bags, 8½ fathoms long,	Bundorg and Grabanalt nets.
1	Net, 150 yards—first pole from shore, 12 yards, last do., 150 yards,	Ballygelagh net.
12	Leader, 500 feet, net, 66 feet,	Flagstaff net.
88	Not exceeding 240 yards length,	—
26	Leader, 240 feet; length of net, 92 feet,	Ringabella net.
86	Length, 60 yards,	Cushkeny net.
119	Length, 136 feet—such measurement not to extend said fixed engine beyond the low water mark of ordinary spring tides	Bennett's Court stake net.
13	South side, 677 feet, east side, 204½ feet; Fish Pass south side, 2¼ feet; open at end in river, 4½ feet,	Castlebellingham weir.
18	Leader, 480 feet, bag, 42 feet; first pole, 300 feet from fixed point on shore,	Drughanstown net.
115	Leader, 30 fathoms long; head, 9 fathoms,	St. Dunstan's Well net.
4	Leader, 240 feet; net, 54 feet,	Rush.
127	Leader not exceeding 50 fathoms, and head 3 fathoms long,	—
81	Length, 120 yards,	Lecanne net.
118	Leaders not exceeding 80 yards each in length, and the heads 24 yards in length and 10 yards in width,	Hore Head nets
121	Length not exceeding 95 yards,	Crane fixed net.
17	Weir, 190 feet; H W M town-pole, 90 feet,	Shannon Lawn weir.
24	Wing, 42 yards; alib wing, 44 yards,	Aylerosbeg weir.
28	188 feet; 18 feet eye,	Bunratty weir
31	660 feet,	Doonmore weir.
32	1,254 feet,	Doonbeg weir
35	406 yards long,	Clonnamon weir.
36	The leader, 274 feet long; and head, 50 feet long and 19 feet wide,	Mount Shannon weir.
37	The first or shore leader 167 yards long, the head 20 yards long and 14½ yards wide. The second leader 126 yards long, and the second head 20 yards long and 14½ yards wide.	Millpark weir.
38	The first or shore leader, 154 yards long, first head, 20 yards long and 14½ yards wide. The second leader, 130 yards long; second head, 20 yards long and 14½ yards wide	Laakambaloe weir.
39	The leader 120 yards long, and the head 20 yards long by 14½ yards wide,	Lakyle weir.
40	The leader 60 yards long, and the head 26 yards long and 7 yards wide,	Lynch's Point weir.
41	The leader 115 yards long, and the head 20 yards long and 12 yards wide,	Park Hough weir.
42	The leader 78 yards long, and the head 30 yards long and 9 yards wide,	Poulnagalhy weir.
43	The leader 80 yards long, and the head 28 yards long and 11 yards wide,	Woodpoint weir.
44	The first leader 498 feet long; first head 45½ feet Second leader, 224 feet long; second head, 73½ feet. Third leader, 242 feet long, third head, 72 feet, and the fourth leader, 272½ feet long; fourth head, 73 feet.	Long Rock weir.
45	Leader, 49½ yards long; and head, 33 yards long,	Killacolla weir.
48	The first leader, 169 yards long; first head, 34 yards long. Second leader, 111 yards long; second head, 34 yards long	Kilmacre Point weir.
49	The first leader, 382 feet long; first head, 39 feet long and 13 feet wide. Second leader, 288 feet long; second head, 74 feet long and 16½ feet wide. Third leader, 108 feet long; head, 97 feet long and 17 feet wide	Carrowbanebeg weir.
52	Entire length, 524 yards,	Carrigane weir.
53	Entire length, 167 yards,	Kylatallin weir.

Into certificate 100

CERTIFICATES granted up to 31st December, 1879, for Fixed

No.	Place.	Name of Person to whom Certificate granted.	Date of Certificate.	District to which Net attached.	Description of Fixed Net.
54	Shannon,	Baron Monteagle,	11 February, 1870,	Limerick,	1 Stake Net,
55	Ditto,	Ditto,	Ditto,	Ditto,	1 Ditto,
56	Ditto,	Ditto,	Ditto,	Ditto,	1 Ditto,
57	Ditto,	Ditto,	Ditto,	Ditto,	1 Ditto,
58	Ditto,	Thomas Sandes,	12 March, 1870,	Ditto,	1 Ditto,
57	Ditto,	Robert Leahy,	16 January, 1871,	Ditto,	1 Ditto,
58	Ditto,	Ditto,	Ditto,	Ditto,	1 Ditto,
59	Ditto,	Thomas Sandes,	Ditto,	Ditto,	1 Ditto,
101	Ditto,	Lord Annelly,	10 November, 1871,	Ditto,	1 Ditto,
102	Ditto,	Ditto,	Ditto,	Ditto,	1 Ditto,
103	Ditto,	R. W. C. Barres,	11 November 1871,	Ditto,	1 Ditto,
104	Ditto,	Colonel Vandeleur,	10 November, 1871,	Ditto,	1 Ditto,
105	Ditto,	Ditto,	11 November, 1871,	Ditto,	2 Ditto,
106	Ditto,	Ditto,	10 November, 1871,	Ditto,	1 Ditto,
107	Ditto,	Beauman Cox,	11 November, 187	Ditto,	1 Ditto,
190	Ditto,	Randal Borough,	12 May, 1877,	Ditto,	1 Ditto,
122	Ditto,	Robert Leahy,	24 April, 1878,	Ditto,	2 Ditto,
123	Shannon, off Scattery Island,	Marcus Keane,	31 January, 1879,	Ditto,	3 Ditto,
124	Shannon,	William Creagh Hickie,	Ditto,	Ditto,	1 Ditto,
125	Shannon, off Carrig Island,	Charles Sandes,	7 March, 1879,	Ditto,	1 Ditto,
16	Ballycotton Bay,	John Litton,	31 October, 1865,	Lismore,	1 Big Net,
26	River Blackwater,	John Neil and William Haceway,	11 January, 1868,	Ditto,	1 Stake Net,
64	Ditto,	Trustees, Provincial Bank,	15 February, 1872,	Ditto,	1 Stake Weir,
23	Ditto,	Hon C W Moore Smyth,	21 June 1871,	Ditto,	1 Ditto,
30	Lough Foyle,	The Irish Society,	2 January, 1866,	Londonderry,	1 Stake Net,
31	Ditto,	Ditto,	Ditto,	Ditto,	1 Ditto,
32	Ditto,	Ditto,	Ditto,	Ditto,	1 Ditto,
30	Sea off co. Donegal,	George Young,	27 April, 1868,	Ditto,	1 Bag Net,
33	Ditto,	Ditto,	6 October, 1863,	Ditto,	1 Ditto,
34	Ditto,	Ditto,	Ditto,	Ditto,	1 Ditto,
53	Magilligan Strand,	Sir H. H. Bruce, bart.	2 May, 1870,	Ditto,	1 Ditto,
76	Sea off coast, co. Londonderry,	Alexander Shuldham, A W. White, and R. J. Broughton,	11 May, 1870,	Ditto,	4 Fixed draft nets,
77	Ditto,	John Cromie,	Ditto,	Ditto,	3 Ditto,
66	Magilligan Strand,	Sir H. Bruce, bart ,	23 April, 1871,	Ditto,	1 Ditto,
84	Ditto,	James McGowery,	15 February, 1871,	Ditto,	1 Ditto,
95	Ditto,	William Lorton,	Ditto,	Ditto,	1 Ditto,
96	River Foyle,	The Irish Society,	Ditto,	Ditto,	1 Ditto,
97	Sea off co. Sligo,	Ormsby Jones,	4 November, 1867,	Sligo,	1 Bag Net,
99	Ditto,	Hon. A. E. M. Ashley,	30 October, 1879,	Ditto,	1 Ditto,
91	Sligo River,	Abraham Martin,	20 February, 1871,	Ditto,	2 Fixed draft nets,
100	Drumcliffe River,	William Petrie,	13 April, 1879,	Ditto,	1 Ditto,
19	Barrow, otherwise Suir, Nore, and Barrow conjoined,	Lord Templemore,	4 December, 1863,	Waterford,	1 Head Weir,
46	Waterford Harbour,	A. N. O'Neill,	8 February, 1870,	Ditto,	1 Stake Net,
47	Ditto,	Ditto,	Ditto,	Ditto,	1 Ditto,
51	King's Channel,	Ditto,	Ditto,	Ditto,	2 Ditto,

RESULT of INQUIRIES held by the INSPECTORS of IRISH FISHERIES into the Legality or Illegality of

No.	Where Fixed Net situated.	Description of Fixed Net.	Name of Person maintaining and using Fixed Net.	Name of Owner of Fixed Net, or of Land to which Net attached.	Name of Townland to which Net attached.	Parish.
406	Sea creek, co. Mayo,	2 Bag nets,	Chas S S Diskins,	Chas. S. S. Diskins,	Bellanglasse,	Achill,
407	Sea coast, co. Sligo,	1 Do.,	Hon, A E M Ashley,	Hon A E M. Ashley,	Mullaghmore,	Ahamlish,
408	Do.,	1 Fixed draft net	Do.	Do.	Kilkilloge,	Do.,
409	River Erne,	1 Stake net,	R L Moore, S M. Moore, and S. M. Alexander,	R L Moore, S M Moore, and S M Alexander,	Furnee,	Inishmacsaint,
410	Kenmare Bay,	1 Bag net	Francis C Bland,	Francis C Bland,	Illaunsla, Derryquin,	Kilcrohane,
611	Dingle Bay,	4 Fixed draft nets	Lord Bervey Ventry,	Lord Baron Ventry,	Cromane Lower,	Killorgin,

APPENDIX, No 18.

QUANTITY of SALMON exported to undermentioned places in England, from Ireland, from 1st January to 31st December, 1879

No. of Boxes of 168 lbs. each

London,	5,763
Nottingham,	9,608
Bradford,	3,711
Manchester,	5,976
Sheffield,	4,503
Wolverhampton,	3,215
Leeds,	3,899
Liverpool,	8,672
Birmingham,	6,609

computed at 1s 3d. per lb   Value delivered at foregoing places would be £482,240 12s. 6d

Total, 1879,	45,039	
Total, 1878,	44,637½ Increase, 401½.	

No. 16—*continued.*

Engines for fishing for Salmon or Trout—*continued.*

No	Particulars of Size, &c.	Observations
54	Leader, 200 feet long; head, 84 feet long,	Foyne's Island (south) weir.
55	Leader, 187 feet long; head, 80 feet long, and 18 feet 6 inches wide.	Foyne's Island (north) weir.
56	The first leader, 566 feet long; first head 103 feet long and 14 feet wide. Second leader, 285 feet long; second head, 96 feet long and 19 feet wide.	Durnish weir.
57	The first leader, 200 feet long; first head, 40 feet long and 33 feet wide. Second leader, 210 feet long; second head, 95 feet long, 18 feet wide	Mount Trenchard weir.
56	Shoe—327 feet from high-water mark.	Coolnameenagh weir.
87	Length, 117 yards,	Tarbert net.
58	Length, 67 yards,	Kilpedogue net.
59	Length, 82 yards 2 feet,	Rahpana net.
101	Leader, 110 yards long,	Saver weir.
102	Leader, 70 yards long,	Battery weir.
104	Leader, 106 yards long; head, 36 yards, and 8 wide,	Poulaudurroe weir.
104	Leader, 60 yards long; head, 7 yards long,	Ayelvarroe or Ballynote weed weir.
106	E. Weir, leader, 76 yards long; head, 17 yards—W. Weir leader, 96 yards long; 3 heads each, 17 yards long	Carrowdotnamintera & western weirs.
106	Leader, 30 yards long; head, 17 yards long,	Cohnamtown weir.
107	5 leaders, each 120 yards, and 5 heads, each 17 yards long,	Clarsfield weir.
120	4 heads, whole length not to exceed 550 yards, measurements not to extend fixed engines below low water of ordinary spring tides.	Shannamagh weir.
122	No. 1, 112 yards in length, and No. 2, 90 yards in length, measurements not to extend fixed engines below low water of ordinary spring tides.	
124	C net, 300 yards long, D net, 155 yards long; and E net, 525 yards long,	Scattery Island weirs.
125	Three heads; the whole length not exceeding 350 yards,	Closmanus weir.
126	300 yards long,	Carry Island weir.
16	271 feet,	Ballyzaikan net.
29	185 feet, Leader,	Scar weir.
96	Length of Shore-arm, 79 feet; body of Weir, 88 feet; Flood-arm, 15 feet; large yard, width, 18 feet; Fish pocket, width, 17 feet.	Steel weir.
99	Leader, 81 feet long, head, 106 feet—Ballinatrey Weir,	Ballynatrey weir.
20	In-pole of Shore Leader to outer pole of same 183 feet, out-pole of do. to do. of Ebb Leader, 83 feet; out-pole of chambers of said channel yards, 17 feet.	The Creek weir.
21	In-pole of Shore Leader to outer pair of same, 196 feet, out-pole of do. to do. of Flood Leader, 112 feet, out-pole of chambers of said channel yards, 92 feet.	The Shell Rock weir.
22	In-pole of Shore Leader to outer pole of same, 262 feet; out pole of do. to do. of Flood Leader, 152 feet,	The Chapel Brook weir.
30	3rd feet, inner to outer pole,	Clogga net.
33	Leader, 270 feet; bag, 78 feet,	Bumpagoe net.
34	Ditto, ditto,	Carrickafaul net.
53	Leader, 313 yards long; head, 17 yards long,	Ballymacbery net.
76	3—820 yards in length; and 3—140 yards in length,	Crossereagh and Tallaghmurney nets.
77	2 nets, 130 yards long, and 1—122 yards long,	Mallaghacall nets.
82	Net exceeding 240 yards length,	
94	160 yards long,	
95	150 yards long,	
96	From 100 to 200 yards long,	
97	Leader, 110 yards, length of net, 90 yards,	Streedagh net.
29	365 feet, inner to outer pole,	Mullaghmore net.
91	Each net exceeding 135 yards length,	Drumcliffe net.
108	150 yards in length,	Buttermilk Castle weir.
18	Shore wing, 225 feet; channel wing, 84 feet, space between shore wing and rock, 45 feet,	
46	The first leader, 283 yards long; and the second leader, 436 yards 1 foot long,	Knockvalesh weir.
47	The first leader, 552 yards long; second leader, 306 yards 1 foot long,	Woodstown weir.
51	Lower weir—leader, 68 yards long; upper weir—leader, 33 yards long. The head or pocket of the former extending from west to east 34 yards in breadth, and the latter extending from west to east 32 yards.	King's Channel weirs (3).

No. 17.

Fixed Nets erected or used for catching Salmon in Ireland, during the year 1879, and to 31st March, 1880.

No	Barony.	County.	Judgment of Inspectors.	Date of Judgment.	Whether Judgment of Inspectors appealed against	Result of Appeal to Court of Queen's Bench
406	Burrishoole,	Mayo,	Legal,	19th Sept., 1879.	—	—
407	Carbury,	Sligo,	Do.	24th Sept., 1879.	—	—
408	Do.	Do.	Do.	Do.	—	—
409	Tirhugh,	Donegal,	Do.	25th Sept., 1879.	—	—
410	Dunkerron South	Kerry,	Do.	14th Nov., 1879.	—	—
411	Traghanacmy,	Do.	Adjourned,	—	—	—

APPENDIX, No. 19.

QUANTITY of SALMON consigned to Billingsgate Market, from Ireland, during the year 1879.

5,762 large boxes, average weight 150 lbs. each, at 1s. 3d. per lb., equal to £54,018 15s.

APPENDIX No. 20.

RIVERS, the Mouths of which have been defined or re-defined in 1879, and to 31st March, 1880, making, with those enumerated in previous Reports, 154 in number.

District	Name of River.	District	Name of River.
Limerick,	Mill.	Limerick,	Ardcloony.
Do.,	Kilnastulla.	Do.,	Maikaar.
Do.,	Blackwater.	Waterford,	*Owenduff or Bannow.

APPENDIX, No. 21.

RIVERS, the TIDAL and FRESH WATER BOUNDARIES of which have been defined to 31st March, 1879.

River.	Boundary	Date
Adrigole,	Adrigole Bridge,	10th June, 1871.
Annagh,	Ballinhagga Bridge, between the townlands of Dough and Annagh,	27th November, 1878.
Annagearagh	The barrier of stones at seaward side of Lough Donnell, between the townlands of Cloghaunahy and Clooaingurraun.	27th November, 1878.
Bandon,	The Bridge at Innoshannon, known as the Innoshannon Bridge,	19th January, 1865.
Bann,	The Down Stream end of Fishing Weir, known as the Cutts,	12th November, 1875.
Barrow,	The lowest Weir or Dam used for navigation purposes, near St. Mullins, in county Carlow,	16th March, 1864.
Blackwater,	A straight line drawn due north across river at townland boundary between townlands of Ballynelligan Glebe and Ballynawan	15th March, 1879.
Boyne,	Eastern Point of Grove Island at Oldbridge,	9th April, 1868.
Bride,	Tallow Bridge Quay,	24th January, 1874.
Caragh,	The Curragh Bridge, being the bridge immediately seaward of the Salmon Weir,	19th January, 1866.
Cashiboy,	Carnyboy Bridge,	10th June, 1871.
Dee,	Williamtown Weir,	20th May, 1872.
Deel or Askeaton,	Askeaton Bridge,	20th November, 1870.
Eske,	Foot Bridge above Donegal Bridge,	17th July, 1862.
Fane,	The Railway Bridge across said River,	16th May, 1871.
Feale,	The Road leading through Killarnin from the Road leading from Listowel to Enniscouch by a line drawn in continuation of said Killarnin Road across River.	4th October, 1875.
Fergus,	The Bridge commonly known as the New Bridge, immediately below the Club House, at Ennis,	9th April, 1864.
Finisk,	A straight line drawn in a westerly direction across river at townland boundary between townlands of Qumalen and Bewley.	15th March, 1879.
Galey or Gwebe,	The Stream called and known by the name of the Gerah-Glenn, between the townlands of Gortnacrowneen and Derrunineeshen.	4th October, 1875.
Glengarriff,	Cromwell's Bridge,	10th June, 1871.
Glashaninn,	The bridge across river known as the Lutch Bridge near Cappoquin,	15th March, 1879.
Glyde,	Lynn's Weir,	20th May, 1872.
Gosub,	A straight line drawn in a north easterly direction across river from a point on townland of Dunmore, at the road leading to Villierstown, to a point on the townland of Coolahet.	15th March, 1879.
Grvagagh,	A straight line drawn in a north westerly direction across river at the townland boundary between the townlands of Raheen and Ballyhenry.	15th March. 1879.
Iveh,	Adare Bridge,	1st February, 1866.
Leane,	The shallow at the head of the Pool, commonly called the Cat Pool,	26th July, 1865.
Lee,	The Weir or Dam at the Water Works of Cork, known as the Water Works Weir,	12th August, 1864.
Leeky,	The bridge across river known as the Ballyheeny Bridge,	10th March, 1879.
Laffey,	The Weir or Dam on said river known as the Island Bridge Weir,	12th August, 1864.
Maigue,	The Bridge across river immediately outside and seaward of the Adare Demesne,	19th August, 1864.
Maine,	A straight line drawn across river at right angles with its course at the boundary between the townlands of Godsheva and Ballyfannan.	29th July, 1865.
Mealogh or Dunamanark	Wooden Bridge at Dunnamark Mill,	10th June, 1871.
Moy,	The foot of the falls immediately below the Weirs at Ballina,	26th July, 1865.
Nore,	The Innistmeague Bridge,	16th March, 1864.
Owvena or Bally-hokey	The Ballyhikey Bridge on the High Road,	10th June, 1871.
Shannon,	The Weir or Dam known as the Cnhally Mill Weir,	9th April, 1864.
Slaney,	The Castle Bridge near Newcastle,	23rd August, 1868.
Slaney,	Enniscorthy Bridge,	1st February, 1864.
Sligo or Garvogue,	The Mill Dam above Victoria Bridge, in town of Sligo,	11th February, 1871.
Snave or Coomhola,	Snave Bridge,	10th June, 1871.
Suir,	A line drawn across river at and opposite to the most up-stream part of the Coolnamuck Weir,	16th March, 1864.
Tahilla,	The mouth of river as defined 21st November, 1875, by a straight line drawn in a north easterly direction across said river from a point on townland of Tahilla to a point on townland of Derrynaunknight	5th February, 1879.
Tourig,	The bridge known as the Two Mile Bridge,	15th March, 1879

* Re defined 10th June, 1879.

DUBLIN: Printed by ALEX. THOM & Co., 87, 88, & 89, Abbey-street,
The Queen's Printing Office.
For Her Majesty's Stationery Office.

www.ingramcontent.com/pod-product-compliance
Lightning Source LLC
Chambersburg PA
CBHW022021080426
42733CB00007B/667